T0117931

How to Change Your Mindset
for the Better
....
Soar with the Eagles
....
and Live the Life of Your Dreams

UNLEASH
YOUR INNER
WARRIOR

BRAD C. WENNEBERG

New York

Unleash Your Inner Warrior

How to Change Your Mindset for the Better, Soar With the Eagles,
and Live the Life of Your Dreams

Copyright 2009 Brad C. Wenneberg. All rights reserved.

No part of this publication may be reproduced or transmitted in any form or by any means, mechanical or electronic, including photocopying and recording, or by any information storage and retrieval system, without permission in writing from the author or publisher (except by a reviewer, who may quote brief passages and/or short brief video clips in a review.)

Disclaimer: The Publisher and the Author make no representations or warranties with respect to the accuracy or completeness of the contents of this work and specifically disclaim all warranties, including without limitation warranties of fitness for a particular purpose. No warranty may be created or extended by sales or promotional materials. The advice and strategies contained herein may not be suitable for every situation. This work is sold with the understanding that the Publisher is not engaged in rendering legal, accounting, or other professional services. If professional assistance is required, the services of a competent professional person should be sought. Neither the Publisher nor the Author shall be liable for damages arising herefrom. The fact that an organization or website is referred to in this work as a citation and/or a potential source of further information does not mean that the Author or the Publisher endorses the information the organization or website may provide or recommendations it may make. Further, readers should be aware that internet websites listed in this work may have changed or disappeared between when this work was written and when it is read.

ISBN 978-1-60037-533-0

MORGAN · JAMES
THE ENTREPRENEURIAL PUBLISHER

Morgan James Publishing, LLC
1225 Franklin Ave., STE 325
Garden City, NY 11530-1693
Toll Free 800-485-4943
www.MorganJamesPublishing.com

In an effort to support local communities, raise awareness and funds, Morgan James Publishing donates one percent of all book sales for the life of each book to Habitat for Humanity. Get involved today, visit **www.HelpHabitatForHumanity.org**.

This book is dedicated to my wife, Bonnie. Through all the ups and downs, she has always been by my side. Our love and passion for each other and for enriching others' lives has been a blessing. From humble beginnings, we have built a wonderful family and life together. Without Bonnie's support and belief in me and in my dreams, I would not be the man I am today!

With Gratitude and Love,

Brad

Acknowledgments

With all things in life, it requires assistance, guidance, mentorship, friends, and other numerously talented people to be successful—individuals working for a common goal, dream, and purpose. I see this phenomenon in action daily on my *dojo* floor at American Martial Arts Academy, where my students must work synergistically with their instructors in order to achieve the ultimate goal of Black Belt. Likewise, it is a collaboration of highly talented, skilled, and dedicated people that have made *Unleash Your Inner Warrior* a reality.

I am truly grateful to my wife, Bonnie, for encouraging me to write this book, and to Leo and Shirley Cohen, my in-laws, for helping me to realize my true potential. To my children, Sheri and Jason, for their continued trust and faith in me, and to my brother Hugh for his laughter, friendship, and faith.

Special thanks to Dr. Debra Holland, Karen Spaeder, Rylan Brenner, and many others who assisted in the many drafts, edits, and rewrites that helped this book go from concept to completion. Thanks, too, to my publishing company, Morgan James, for having faith in the message of the warrior.

I also thank Alex Alaev, Dr. Jeffrey S. Bodwin, Jeff Shore, Caleb Beller, Nikhil Joshi, and other fellow karate friends, students, and colleagues who have inspired me and are living the life of a warrior.

Another special thanks to the fellowship of Alcoholics Anonymous. I have gained wisdom and strength from the twelve steps and twelve traditions outlined in AA and have made many friends who have saved my life and helped me to become a spiritual warrior.

I especially thank Dr. Marvin Rofsky, the therapist who saved me from myself. Without him, I wouldn't be here to pass on the message of the warrior.

Most of all, I thank God for gentle and loving guidance. By doing God's will, I have found peace of body, mind, and soul.

Testimonials

- "I've seen Brad go from being near death to becoming a successful teacher, mentor, and leader both in and out of his karate academy. His passion, determination, and ability to carry the message of hope to others have never been more evident than in *Unleash Your Inner Warrior*. I have no doubt that this book will empower thousands with a newfound passion for life." *–Dr. Jeffrey S. Bodwin, M.D., 4th Degree Black Belt*

- "*Unleash Your Inner Warrior* is more than just a self-help book; it's a hands-on guide to achieving your dreams. As one of Brad's martial arts students and mentees who has personally applied his success principles, I can attest that his system—when followed correctly—will allow you to maximize your own potential." *–Karen E. Spaeder, Former Managing Editor of Entrepreneur Magazine and Founder of Rain Frog Apparel*

- "I recommend anyone who is currently in or one day wishes to be in a leadership role take courses from Brad C. Wenneberg. I am a consultant in the field of management and professional development. Brad's success coaching has all the elements of a complete and thorough leadership and self-development program." *–Shirley Fox, 1st Degree Black Belt and Management Consultant*

- "Since mentoring with Brad C. Wenneberg, I now have the knowledge and confidence to achieve my goals. I may never open my own martial arts studio, but the skills he has taught me has helped improve my professional and personal life tremendously. I recommend this school and his services to anyone who wishes to learn how to be successful." *–Arkadi Alaev, 2nd degree Black Belt and Founder of AAA Global*

- "I have gained a new outlook on my future and have enhanced my self-esteem and my earning power as a result of Brad's fantastic success coaching. It has been a great help in my business and personal life; in fact, as a result of the mentoring, I was able to set new goals and begin my own business career. I highly recommend this book to anyone looking to boost their own careers and their enjoyment in life." *–Jeffrey Shore, 2nd Degree Black Belt and Owner of Star Service*

- "Brad has given me great courage and hope. Thank you! My experience with his success coaching has been one of the best leadership-building programs that I have ever encountered. Unlike other courses, the coaching provides a well-rounded opportunity to learn in-depth leadership skills and styles. Brad's success coaching has helped me to become a leader in the school band, as well as at church, and has helped guide my path through high school and into my Naval career. His coaching is for anyone who is interested in learning simple yet effective leadership and success skills that can be applied to just about any situation." *–Andrew Barragan, 1st degree Black Belt and Yeoman Third Class, United States Navy*

- "As a motivational speaker, business developer, and director of a nonprofit foundation, I have spent many years studying and reviewing success-oriented books and CDs. What I appreciate most about Brad's book is that he opens up his life by revealing his and his family's successes and failures while using success principles as a discussion framework. I found these life lessons compelling and applaud Brad and his presentation of them." *–Jeffrey M. Israel, M.D., Director of the FACES Foundation and Founder of ICAN Global*

Foreword

I've known Brad C. Wenneberg since 1996, ever since I wandered into his martial arts academy to sign up for classes. At the time, I just wanted to learn a little karate because I'd always loved *The Karate Kid* movies. I had no idea of the challenging and wonderful path I was about to embark upon.

Although I had always played sports and, in the three years before starting karate, had taken ballet classes, I wasn't a fighter. Just the opposite, I'm a psychotherapist, a healer. It went against my natural instincts to spar. I struggled during my first year, sometimes tearfully as I tried to reprogram myself to be more aggressive. When someone would hit or kick me, I'd instinctively think, *Ow. Can't we just talk about this?*

I confessed my sensitivity to Brad. I told him about the tears and reluctance to fight. He sat with me and gently told me he didn't care if I cried my way to Black Belt. It was fine with him; he'd support me all the way. He designed a training routine with two understanding instructors that would push me, without overwhelming me.

And it worked. I began to relax and enjoy learning martial arts. Brad's dedication, charisma, and wicked sense of humor made for interesting and inspirational classes. Outside of the *dojo*, Brad and I became mutual mentors and friends.

As time passed, I gradually became more confident with my sparring, until during the matches in my Black Belt promotion, my inner warrior broke through, and I *fought*. Afterwards, my amazement at my unexpected performance was made even more special by the look of pride on Brad's face. Later, he hugged me and said, "I always knew you could do it."

I became an example of Brad's philosophy—that becoming a Black Belt is not about being held to an external standard of excellence. It's about becoming the best Black Belt *you* can be. Nor is it only about physically learning the fighting techniques, katas, and traditions, but about overcoming any blocks that hold you back from attaining *any* of your life goals—unleashing your inner warrior by transforming your mindset.

Along my path to my first degree black belt and beyond, I witnessed Brad's philosophy in action many times. I've seen hyper or aggressive children, shy teenagers, mentally and/or physically challenged individuals, and overweight, out of shape adults change and grow. As they worked toward achieving their black belts, they became physically fit, gained confidence in themselves, and undertook new challenges in other areas of their lives.

Brad has built his karate academy into one of the most successful in California. And the principles he uses to succeed can be implemented with any other business. Yet, even more important than his financial success is his commitment to helping individuals change and grow. I've frequently heard his motto: "A warrior is one who serves."

I've also watched Brad apply his training techniques to his own life. He has demonstrated the value of positive goals, persistence, and commitment by working through some trouble spots in his marriage and overcoming a failed business venture that left him deeply in debt.

This is a man who has been to the dark depths and fought back, each time emerging stronger. He has lived the precepts he teaches and now shares them with you.

In *Unleash Your Inner Warrior*, Brad C. Wenneberg tells a starkly honest account of his personal story. He shares the wisdom and experience gathered from life-long (and often hard-learned) lessons, which he has distilled into an engaging book that can ultimately help *anyone* (regardless if she or he practices martial arts or not) evolve into a true warrior, make lasting personal changes, and find a richer, more fulfilling life.

My hope is that you will get as much from this book as I have from my years of working with Brad Wenneberg. *Now* is the time to unleash the warrior within you and live the life of your dreams.

Debra Holland, PhD, MST (Marriage, Family and Child Therapist)
Corporate Crisis/Grief Counselor, Entertainment Industry Consultant
2nd Degree Black Belt
Author, *Rules of Engagement: How to Have a Boundary Setting Conversation With a Difficult Person*
www.drdebraholland.com

Contents

Introduction

The year was 1978. I was twenty-five, desperate and full of shame, lying sleepless on a warm spring evening at 3 AM. I reached to my right and opened the nightstand drawer, took out my police service revolver, put the muzzle to my right temple, and without hesitation pulled the trigger.

In my five years as a police officer, never once had I doubted the integrity of my .38 Magnum. At that moment, however, I knew it had failed me—or rather my wife had saved me from ending my own life.

Bonnie had awakened and grabbed hold of me, snatching the revolver from my hand. The next thing I recall was awakening to the reality of being strapped to a bed in the local hospital. Later, Bonnie told me she had unloaded my service revolver before she went to bed that fateful night. I asked her why, especially as she hadn't touched my pistol in the past. She replied, "I had a gut feeling something was wrong, and I followed my instinct."

Screaming, yelling, and tugging violently at my restraints, I cried and pleaded to be let loose so I could finish what I had started—to destroy what I had become. As I became more and more exhausted, my pleas became cries for help. I didn't really want to die, yet I was afraid of living as I had been.

Hour after hour, I stared at the ceiling, pleading for answers. I wanted someone to come to my rescue, to offer me the magic pill that would make me well. I felt hopeless and helpless, until suddenly I felt a calm come over me. And even though I was alone, I heard a voice say, "Remember when you were six years old, passionate and determined about life, and you promised to be successful and happy? It is time for you to once again find your purpose in life and live to do great things!"

In the morning, I told the nurse that she could untie the restraints— that I had ceased my fight for death, and had chosen instead to live.

From that moment on, I was determined I would never again live my life as a drunk. I knew then that nothing—not a bottle, not anything—could stand in the way of my dreams. I was a man with a mission, a purpose, a vision of the man I knew I could become.

At that point, I began a career in the insurance industry, and I worked there successfully for ten years. I was a member of the Million Dollar Round Table and had developed a thriving business. Meanwhile, I began to teach karate at a local health club and found I loved it. I was a changed man, yet my journey was just beginning.

In 1992, I was still happily married to Bonnie, and we had two wonderful children, Sheri and Jason. I decided that even though I had achieved great success in the insurance industry, I was ready to fulfill my vision in life. I decided I was going to open my own karate studio and build it into the finest teaching institution in the world.

With complete support from my family, I began the next part of my journey in August, 1992. Since then, I have learned through trial and error, study, mentorship, and determination how to achieve massive success financially, emotionally, personally, and spiritually. Today I am making a difference in the world by helping thousands of people of all ages to maximize their potential.

What I have learned since that day when life was unbearable has transformed me into a responsible and respected member of society. I have learned the lessons necessary to unleash the power of the warrior within.

In this book, we will travel through my personal experiences of tragedy and survival, including the lessons learned and the way to apply these lessons in everyday life.

The challenges I faced and overcame should strike a personal note in everyone who reads this book. My hope is that these lessons and the solutions to the problems I faced will transform your life as well so that you take action *before* some tragic, life-altering event comes your way. We all have something we wish to change, whether that would mean losing weight, getting fit, bettering our relationships, making more income—the list goes on. It is not enough, however, simply to want change or even to make some so-called changes in our lives. Give me a twenty-dollar bill, and I will give you four five-dollar bills in exchange. I have changed your twenty into fives, but it still adds up to twenty.

I tried over and over again to make positive changes, but all I ended up doing was changing from one poor habit to another or just white-knuckling some "change." I discovered this was temporary and self-defeating.

True transformation of my mind, body, and spirit took proper mentorship and my willingness to be teachable. Until I was completely willing to do whatever it took to transform completely, I was doomed for failure.

It was my own willingness to transform that has allowed my martial arts/life skills school to become one of the largest and most successful martial arts businesses in the world, grossing millions of dollars—but better yet, being of service to others. A warrior is one who serves.

Through specific success principles—along with a vision and a passion—I have achieved success and freedom. In doing so, I have made a difference in the world, and I've changed the pattern in my family from one of negativity and just getting by to one of freedom.

This book is meant for one purpose and one purpose only: to guide you into a mindset that sets you free to achieve your dreams and your vision and to ensure you a legacy of greatness. We deserve to live the life of our dreams, and nobody should ever be allowed to steal our dreams away from us. It is time for you to say, "The buck stops with me!"

I invite you to join me on this journey. Open your heart and your soul to experience and absorb a new "warrior" concept of life. Through my experiences I have developed a strategy for unleashing the power of the warrior within!

Chapter 1

Opening the Door to Greatness—
Dream, Vision, Purpose, Legacy

Unleashing my inner warrior was a challenge to me in every way: a challenge to the way I do business, to my habits, to my self-esteem, and to my comfort zones. It is a challenge to learn what I *need* to know, not what I *want* to know. It challenges me to act instead of just listen, and it challenges me to leave the past behind and move forward.

Let me give you a little history as to how I was able to determine my purpose. At age fifteen, I got my first job as a teacher of handball at the YMCA, and I loved it. Soon after, I took a job at a shoe company and excelled in my sales ability as I truly enjoyed my interaction with customers. I became a manager at a store of a large shoe company and found I enjoyed all aspects of the operation except for the detailed administrative part of the business. At twenty-one, I began my career as a police officer in which I loved dealing with people, especially training new officers and conducting community workshops. After my medical retirement from the police department, I went on to be a private investigator, and I hated it. It was lonely and boring, and it didn't allow me to interact with people. Next, was my insurance career; this was good because once again I dealt with helping people. I also had been taking karate lessons and, as I advanced, I found I loved teaching lower-ranked students.

At this point in my life, I met a gentleman who became my mentor. He asked me some very pointed questions, and the answers changed my life forever. He asked, "What is your purpose in life?" I replied that I really liked teaching and helping people. He then asked what my hobby was, and I said that I taught martial arts part-time—and that I was passionate about what I accomplished through teaching. He advised me, "Quit your insurance business and follow through with your passion."

In 1992, I walked away from insurance and opened my own karate studio, and the rest is history. I have found a way to fulfill my purpose—a purpose larger than self—by teaching and helping others to become the best they can be. By following my passion and working a strategic plan, I have become financially free, emotionally fit, and spiritually enriched. I have also found new passion in my relationships. I am a warrior—one who serves.

It is the first of all problems for a man to find out what kind of work he is to do in this universe.

Thomas Carlyle

I discovered that I do have the choice to be whom and what I want to be—I can soar with the eagles. We all have the freedom and the abilities to live life beyond our wildest dreams. The only difference between those who do and those who don't is a decision followed by accurate thinking and then accurate action.

As a youngster, all I ever heard were variations on "someday our ship will come in (and solve our financial woes)," "those who have money are lucky," or "you need to be born into the right family." I felt I wasn't smart enough, tall enough, or talented enough. I also thought I was doomed by my family's history of mediocrity.

This wasn't acceptable to me, and I decided that somehow I would soar like an eagle. I would make my life a blessing. I was bound and determined to make this my quest even though I had no idea how to make it a reality.

I needed a strategic design for living life to its fullest. I needed to determine my purpose in life and unleash my inner warrior. It was my responsibility to fulfill my purpose in life. I made a commitment for something greater than self. I uncovered my purpose and pledged allegiance to it. I was told that, "If I don't stand for something, I will fall for anything."

So, what is my purpose? I realized my purpose in life is to be a teacher, a leader, a mentor, and an athlete. My purpose is to help as many people as possible to maximize their potential. I find true meaning in looking people eye to eye and being of service. I find joy in helping my students to learn to defend themselves physically, mentally, and spiritually. My dream is being able to help people find their potential and live life with a purpose.

Knowing my purpose is what was missing from my life. Having a purpose was the single most important factor in getting what I wanted out of life!

Nothing is cast in stone except my purpose. Goals may change—purpose, never. Think back to my story: I was the happiest when I was working with and helping people. That is my purpose. However, the professions I've used to fulfill this purpose have varied dramatically from one to the next.

The majority of people are in a job that is not aligned with their life purpose. Maybe they take these jobs because a friend recommended it, it was close to home, their parents directed them that way, or they just got stuck in the rut. People are unhappy with what they do because they aren't doing something they are passionate about and they no longer have a dream. From birth to death, we must decide each day to live with purpose or become willing to settle for mediocrity.

When we know our purpose, the vehicle to fulfill that purpose will show up because we can now clearly see the target. If what you are currently doing doesn't support your purpose, I recommend change. Purpose is solitarily your most important responsibility. In fact, our purpose in life is to live our lives with purpose.

I suggest you take a moment and complete this statement:

My purpose in life is: _____

_____

It is time for us to open the door to greatness and unleash the warrior from within.

Let's talk a moment about "trying." I couldn't just *try* to determine my purpose in life or *try* to plan my life, I had to *do* it! I have discovered that *try* is really a four letter word. I had to scratch *try* from my dictionary and from my vocabulary.

Try is a weasel word. It's for those of us who are not committed to *do*, so we weasel out of doing by "trying" to do. I had to stand up and go ahead, knowing I could either stand up or fail.

Here's a parable: Two frogs are floating down a river on a branch when they notice a huge waterfall ahead. In a panic, one of the frogs decides to jump off to safety. The question becomes: how many frogs go over the falls? The answer: both frogs plunge to their deaths because even though one had decided to jump to safety, he never took action. It's not enough to have good intentions—people have to take action and do it!

When I decided to take control of the direction of change in my life, I designed a plan of action. If I didn't know what I wanted, how would I notice when it showed up?

There is great power in being specific. I call it "specific intentions." When I get specific about what I want and what my mission is, I can then begin to get focus in my life. I have to honor my specific intentions. I have discovered that what I specifically intend to do is what usually gets handled first.

What do I want? I had to ask myself that question a lot, trying to determine what I wanted out of life. What is it that I could do, or have done, that would make me feel good about myself? What would bring me joy, pleasure, and satisfaction? What would serve me as well as others? Only when I figured this out could I design a plan to achieve what I wanted out of life.

To follow a path all one's life without knowing where it really leads,
Such is the behavior of the multitude.

Mencius

I decided that change is nothing to fear, as it is consistent with life. From change springs opportunity, growth, and achievement. When I let it, change nurtures me.

I began to accept change; I learned to manage change; I began to control the progress I made in life. It took courage, effort, and patience to alter my old way of living to a new way. It was not easy to transform my life of self-involvement, negativity, insecurity, and fearfulness into one that would allow me to experience life fully. I began to trust myself that I had chosen the best path and also began to have faith in a higher power greater than myself. I found fulfillment and satisfaction in the acceptance of change. I also discovered that I will never get to where I want to go until I have come from where I've been. If I continue to do what I have always done, I will continue to get what I have always gotten.

In causing change to come about, our greatest power is choice, and our second greatest power is imagination. To begin on the road to greatness, I followed these guidelines and continue to practice them daily:

- ➤ I started with a clear picture in mind of what I would like to have happen.
- ➤ I put my imagination to work constructively.
- ➤ I projected ahead.
- ➤ I visualized my purpose (visualizing is thinking about it and being able to see what hasn't happened yet).
- ➤ I saw myself as a winner.

➢ I imagined how it would look, smell, taste, sound, and feel when I reached my goals.

➢ I remembered to do only "positive" visualization.

➢ I visualized health and imagined wealth. What did I want? I could see it!

➢ I recognized that when I learn to see the invisible, I can do the impossible.

➢ I realized that what I think about and speak about, I bring about.

➢ I warned myself to be careful what I think about—I just might get it!

Without this playing with fantasy, no creative work has ever yet come to birth. The debt we owe to the play of the imagination is incalculable.

Carl Jung

I had to ask myself: how would I be remembered? What did I want my legacy to be? It was all up to me. I had to stop placing blame on outside factors, as my destiny was my responsibility. What has happened in the past doesn't matter, and no one really cares. All that counts is what I decide to do today. Whatever it is I want, whatever my purpose is, I had to decide now to change and have a life directed toward greatness by making the determinations and going through the visualizations I've outlined above.

There is a warrior within all of us! I had to resolve now, at that very minute, that I would no longer fear change or fear the unknown, and that I would take the necessary actions to open my door to greatness.

How Will You Be Remembered?
What Will Your Legacy Be?

Chapter 2

Vision—See It, Feel It, Live It

I grew up with a vision of myself that went like this: I am not good enough, not smart enough, not tall enough, not good looking enough, so I am destined to fail. Basically, I never felt that I fit in. I was always comparing other people's exteriors to what I felt inside. As I said before, we didn't have money so we didn't have the luxuries of life, and we didn't even have what I would call a functional family. It was humiliating to me to constantly have to be using food vouchers and food stamps, and I felt even less of a person afterwards as this was something I took as a personal failure.

I know now that my passion to be a police officer stemmed from two very powerful desires. One was to help others and make a difference in the world. The second was my downfall —I somehow equated the uniform, badge, gun, and power as a validation of my finally "being okay." I subconsciously felt that people would now see me as worthwhile, strong, smart, and valuable. What I found out was that no matter what I wore on the outside, that scared little boy inside was still there.

On Friday evening when I was fifteen, I took my first drink of alcohol. I was with three of my high school friends, and my older brother bought us a fifth of Southern Comfort. I remember each of us filling a tiny cup with this elixir. With my first swallow, I felt the burn as it went down my throat, but within fifteen minutes I was taking the bottle, locking myself in the bowling alley restroom, and gulping it straight from the bottle. As I gazed at myself in the mirror, I felt like I'd been instantly transformed into a lean, mean, fighting machine. I felt taller, smarter, better looking, and invincible. It was the feeling I'd always wanted—the one of confidence and courage.

Two hours later, my friends literally threw me onto the porch of my home while I was projectile vomiting. I remember waking up at three the next afternoon and swearing to my mom I would never drink alcohol again, but in the back of my mind, I couldn't wait to have that feeling again. I know now that the drinking was an artificial and temporary medication that masked my fears and insecurities. The problem was that when I sobered up, there I was once again.

I blamed everyone for my lack of confidence—my mother, father, brothers, and sisters; the police department; my wife; the DMV, the traffic, the weather—you name it, I blamed it. Until I took full responsibility for my actions and made a decision to accept myself for whom and what I was, I was unable to create a new vision and unleash my inner warrior.

In the martial arts, we teach and reteach the basics, the fundamentals. We start out as a new white belt; and one step at a time, we progress to the next level, and eventually reach black belt. Then we return to the novice stage and begin anew. We learn that to become a black belt, we must have a vision of ourselves *as* a black belt. Once we have that vision of being a black belt, we reach it with a designed plan of action and determination that we then implement.

I had to create a new image of myself from scratch. In order for me to break the shackles of the past, I had to begin anew. I hadn't shut the door on the past, but I couldn't live in it. I made a decision and then took appropriate action to change my "way" in every aspect of my life. This certainly takes time, but it is merely a matter of making a decision and taking action.

Was I ready to make that decision? If not, it was suggested that I fake it, but that I *do it now*! That very moment, I decided to let go of all the junk I'd been storing up year after year. I decided to take action and make the appropriate changes. I decided that my life would have meaning. I decided that the buck stops with me. It took nothing more than a decision, then action. I was fed up with being sick and tired. Change is the way of the warrior, so I took action to make it come about.

I didn't say it was easy, but it was simple. I just had to be willing to step out of my comfort zone, to be willing to embrace change and plan to win. I needed to be a champion!

Simple steps I took:

➢ Stop procrastinating.
➢ Determine my purpose and goals and write them down, recognizing knowledge is power.
➢ Resolve now to take some kind of action, however small, as action creates opportunity.
➢ Launch myself towards my goals each and every day. As Yoda said, "Do or do not. There is no try!"
➢ Determine *now* which of my habits were creating a negative vision and replace them with positive habits. Negative habits could include:

    o Drinking
    o Drugs
    o Hellivision
    o Computer overuse
    o Gambling
    o Obsessing
    o Overeating
    o The list goes on and on ….

If anything negative was blocking my way to greatness, I had to remove it from my life in order to move forward. My challenges weren't unique—we have all experienced difficulties in our lives. The difference between the winners and the losers is the willingness to take action and make changes, to create a new and rewarding vision.

I had to abandon all negative concepts of myself and adopt a new set of eyeglasses. These glasses let me look inward to the good I have to offer. With them, I can see that my responsibility is to fulfill my purpose and the greatness of my destiny.

My vision of myself today is one of respect and honor. I am an honest and humble man, a caring and giving person. I am spiritually grounded and a loving husband and father. I am a community leader who does my part for the less fortunate. I am a teacher, and I am a student. I care about you, and I accept me. I understand my weaknesses and my strengths, and most of all I know my purpose in life. I am sober and free from drugs, and I help other addicts to live in recovery. I am the man I have always wanted to be, and I owe this all to some very simple principles for living that required action and a power greater than myself (which I call God) to guide me. I don't say this to impress you, but to impress upon you that it *is* possible.

If I were to die today, I would not regret who and what I have become. I have lived a life beyond my wildest (drunken or sober) dreams. My legacy is something that will live on after my death. And if nothing else, I have learned that by being a warrior, one who serves, great things will come to pass.

I suggest you take out a sheet of blank paper (or use the lines below) and create a new vision of yourself—a loving and confident purpose-driven vision. Be detailed in every area: see it, feel it, smell it. Then, one day at a time, take action towards the image and the vision you wish to become. And keep reading—how it works comes next.

It's in Our Hands—Our Vision, Our Purpose!

_____

_____

_____

_____

_____

_____

_____

_____

_____

_____

_____

_____

_____

_____

_____

_____

_____

_____

_____

Chapter 3

How It Works

I wish that there was a magic formula, a magic pill, or even a clever new and improved angle I could introduce you to, but the principles for success have been consistent from the beginning of time. My dilemma was how I should approach these principles and apply them to my personal passion and purpose in life.

As a martial artist, I am well aware of the "one step at a time" process. Students come into my *dojo* with a passion and dream of one day achieving the level of Black Belt. This is exciting and a worthy goal, but like all things worthy in life, it comes with a price. Sadly, most people are unwilling to pay that price even if doing so would mean fulfilling their purpose in life and making their dreams come true.

Let me explain. New students begin their first day of training as a white belt—a beginner, wide-eyed and full of dreams and expectations. There are a total of twelve levels of advancement for a student to reach black belt, with each step requiring a new commitment and renewed enthusiasm for the dream and the vision. This is the challenge: to keep the fires of passion burning within the students.

We guide our students along a path of challenges that include the physical, mental and spiritual, taking each step only after reviewing where they've been and seeing what is next in their journey to black belt. They take tiny steps marked by a series of rewards and goals achieved. The challenge they face is the same challenges we all face in the real world: staying focused on the target, taking tiny steps forward, and keeping the quest for success always in mind.

Unfortunately, what often happens is the challenges of life, with its everyday ups and downs, sidetrack us, and we lose sight of the target. We get discouraged, and unless we have a clear-cut next step, our dream will be crushed. Hence the need to identify the mission, goal, or dream, then break it down into small, manageable achievements with rewards attached.

For example, karate students reach the green belt level after approximately one year of study. At this point they may find themselves bored, or maybe getting to the black belt seems more difficult than they expected. At this point, we evaluate the rewards associated with success and reestablish their primary purpose, then tailor a program to their individual goals (which may have changed since they entered the studio as a white belt). This process generally reenergizes students, and they are once again on target for a great achievement. We come face to face with similar challenges many times during our journey to greatness in life. Will we step up and do what it takes, or will we fall victim to the challenge and quit at our green belt level?

I have never heard holders of black belts say they wished they had quit and never achieved their dream. In contrast, I've met thousands of people who regret quitting halfway through the challenge. A Black Belt will always tell you that the journey was the joy and the belt was the reward—a reward and a success that all came about because that person didn't quit, but instead stayed on target no matter what.

It is critical for us to have a purpose greater than self and a strong will to achieve. This is always the first step. Keeping the momentum and not getting lost in the hustle and bustle of life is where most of us fall apart.

Success in any aspect of our lives is not for the faint of heart. It is not a matter of luck, heritage, color, religion, or social status—it is a matter of battling the forces that are constantly trying to crush our dreams. We can sit back and let life ride us, or we can stand tall and ride life.

Unfortunately, for so many years I joined in with the quitters of the world. I was one of those excuse makers. Instead of being a positive force in the universe, I was a miserable, complaining, whiny, ego-driven child.

Here is what I had to do to unleash my inner warrior: I had to dispense with all the old ideas and concepts about how to live my life. This included my ideas about being a son, a husband, a father, an employee, an employer, and a friend. I had to become the man I never was. I had to embrace a spiritual life, not necessarily a religious one, but a set of principles that meant I was responsible and accountable to a power greater than myself.

My old ideas had put me exactly where I was, so in order to reach the next higher level, I needed to embrace a new level of understanding and intelligence. I had to be willing to approach change with enthusiasm and excitement as opposed to fear and trepidation. I had to stop blaming my parents, brothers, sisters, and wife. Basically I had blamed everything and everyone for my lack of guts and my stubborn resistance to the truth.

The truth is that my own thinking is limited by the mere fact that I cannot rise above human. Therefore, as an imperfect human being, I had to stop drowning in my own "best thinking" and hitch my wagon to those who could guide me and mentor me to the next level in my journey. I had to stop being so self-centered and full of ego and realize the truth of the statement, "I alone will surely fail, while we together will succeed."

Success at any level requires—even demands—teamwork: a united front, bound and determined for a common cause of good. Whether the success is in our relationships, work, friends, or spirituality, it takes a team effort. Look at any sports team considered great—it is always driven by united and passionate members working together.

Had I continued to believe that my success and happiness was all my doing, I would have remained helpless. I was limited by my own ego and refused to see the truth. I had to let go of this notion and seek out those who were at the next level so I could become a student of life. Success in any aspect of my life is measured by my willingness to be teachable.

IDEA for Success

I   Identify your purpose in life.

D   Make a Decision to do whatever it takes to stay on target.

E   Get Excited and enthusiastic.

A   Take Action.

It sounds so simple! The fact is, it *is* simple, yet we as "great thinkers" like to complicate the uncomplicated. In the upcoming chapters, I will walk you through my IDEA strategies for success.

Chapter 4

Purpose Never Changes—
But Our Direction Must Be Flexible

Purpose never changes, but the way it is accomplished has to ebb and flow with life. I have known since I was a young boy that I loved working with and teaching people. This is my purpose, yet I have achieved it in a variety of different ways.

When he was fifteen, my son, Jason, decided he wanted to play basketball at his high school. Jason was all of 5'2" and ninety pounds. The school he attended was full of all-American athletes with the basketball team being one of the best in the state. Jason was motivated and excited; he was determined to participate in basketball because it fit in with his purpose. He wanted to learn the game and apply to it his martial arts training and teaching.

However, when he and a hundred other students tried out for the team, Jason was one of the first to be cut. But Jason is athletic, analytical, and personable—an unusual combination. As he'd been taught that he must never give up on his purpose and dream, Jason looked for another way of achieving his objective. He went to the team coach and volunteered his services as a team helper. He insisted that by doing so, he could be of benefit to the team and make the coach's job easier. Jason was assigned clean-up duties, asked to videotape practices and games, and basically served as the team gopher.

What the coaches didn't expect was that Jason's purpose was so well-defined that he caught everyone's attention. Not only was he the most enthusiastic member of the team, but he was the hardest worker. He learned the plays and practiced with the players before and after games to help improve their skills and confidence. Soon the coaches allowed Jason to practice with the team on a regular basis, during which he outworked the entire team at each and every practice.

His excitement and his motivation were so apparent that after the second regular season game, Jason was made a permanent member of the team roster. Jason played in several games during the next two seasons. He never made an impact with his scoring; however, his purpose was to participate, learn, grow, and help the team be the best it could be. He did this with his attitude and his enthusiasm. The team was pumped up and went on to be one of the best teams the school had ever had. The coaches and the players fed off of Jason's definite major purpose. The vehicle changed (starting as a helper rather than a player), but he never altered his purpose.

This was another life lesson to me that again supports the notion that purpose is necessary for success and a life of fulfillment. Without purpose, we will never hit our targets because there's nothing for us to aim at.

Several years ago, one of my male adult students enrolled in my Business/Instructors College, a six-month intensive course primarily designed to help students to find their purpose in life and to carry that over to helping others. Jeff is an automobile mechanic—and a very good one at that. For years he had been complaining about working for this particular company, and he had always had a burning desire to own his own shop. Because of the lack of freedom, he was not happy being an employee. He had a vision of one day being his own boss, having his own shop, and developing his own following of satisfied customers.

One day, Jeff walked slowly towards me at the dojo with his head low and his shoulders slumped. As he approached, I thought something dreadful must have occurred as he was usually pretty upbeat. He looked down at the ground and cried that he had been fired from his job. He was now unemployed, which was a difficult situation for someone married with two young boys. He said, "Sensei, this is a disaster for me and my family."

Without hesitation I shouted, "That is the best news I have heard all day. Congratulations! It's your freedom day!"

Jeff quickly looked into my eyes and asked, "What the heck? Are you nuts?"

I snapped backed with positive enthusiasm, "Jeff, you can now follow your dream. You have the opportunity to make good on your purpose." Then I went on to remind him of his clearly stated purpose, which was to own and operate his own repair shop. I suggested he direct his passion and purpose to starting his own shop, building his own business, and creating the life that to that day he'd only dreamed about.

He stared at me for what seemed to be several minutes and shouted, "That's right! It's my turn and I am going for it! Maybe this is the time to get off my butt and do what I have always been meant to do." Today, Jeff owns a very successful auto repair shop. He employs several people, he has a loyal following of customers, and he has never been happier. The moral is the same old story: have a purpose, follow your dreams, and then go for it—it is your right and your duty.

I had to stop the bellyaching and identify my burning desire in life. I had to ask myself: what gets my engine going at full throttle? I took an honest inventory of my life and asked: When was I the happiest? What was I doing at the time? When was I unhappiest, and what was I doing at the time? Where and when and what was I doing when I was most satisfied?

I took an honest and complete appraisal of my marriage, my job, my friends, etc. I had to take some time and decide if I was on the right course for my definite major purpose. Was I the person I'd always wanted to be?

I stopped putting my energy into changing others and figured out what needed to be changed in me. I examined my attitude and my motives. I took control of my direction in life and focused on doing and being a purpose-driven person bent on success in all areas of life.

I had to get fighting mad—I mean *really* mad—to make that choice between success and just surviving. I can tell you I am driven by my need to succeed and to be of service to my fellow human beings. This may seem like a fantasy to you, but to me it is a burning fire that needs to be stoked daily. If I had no burn down to my very soul, then I would not be fulfilling my purpose, and I would be living a life of mediocrity and not of greatness.

Today, Jason has taken that drive, passion, and purpose he showed towards the basketball team and is applying it to teaching martial arts to children and adults of all ages. He also has an Internet business to feed his analytical side and mentors others to achieve financial freedom. The vehicles he uses changes, but his purpose to be of help has never wavered.

By identifying our definite major purpose and setting our sails for the journey, we will live our lives beyond our wildest dreams, do whatever it takes to become the best we can be, and leave a lasting legacy. We must refuse to settle for an average life, as "average" is the mindset of the masses. It creates habits that lead to nowhere. We can either be average or outstanding—this we have control over. We must take control of the things we can and stop worrying about the things out of our control. Life is too short, so let's be all we can be *today*—the choice is ours.

If you are still not sure what your purpose is, take some time and think about what brings you satisfaction on a grander scale. Take some quiet, alone time and see what inspires you. What interactions feel the best to you? What have you always wanted to accomplish? Who inspires you by his or her actions? How do you want to be remembered? If time and money weren't obstacles, what would you like to accomplish? Use the space below to jot down the ideas that come to you as you think about these questions. These answers should help point you in the direction of your purpose.

_____

_____

_____

_____

_____

_____

_____

_____

_____

_____

_____

_____

_____

_____

_____

Now that we have identified our purpose, it is time for a decision.

Chapter 5

I Made the Decision

I had to decide either to stand up or not. I make this decision each and every day. Most decisions are insignificant in the scheme of things, but some are life-changing ones and some may even be life-or-death. Decisions are the substance of our life—either we do or we don't. Making the decision and then fully stepping over the line is what separates the successful from the average.

When a ship carrying only enough fuel to reach its destination sets sail and continues on its course, eventually it reaches the halfway point. Then the captain has a decision to make. If he continues on course, he is totally committed because his vessel will only have enough fuel to reach its destination, as the distance will be too great for it to turn back. Whatever he decides, it will be a final decision.

I used to make decisions but give myself a way out: "I will try it, but if it doesn't work, I will quit." "I will try to eat less, but if I can't do it, I will try again next month." The excuses for taking the easy way out went on and on.

I learned that my decisions must be made with conviction and passion. I must cross the barrier of no return and go for my destination with no excuses, no turning back. Decisions can either be for good or for bad, depending on the circumstances. The important thing is: wrong or right, *make a decision.*

While I was on patrol one evening, a call came out over the radio about an armed robbery. The dispatcher described the suspect as being a white male of about twenty-five with short dark hair who was wearing jeans and a T-shirt and driving a dark-colored Chevy Impala. I was in the vicinity of the robbery, and directly ahead of me was a vehicle matching the description. It turned left and sped off. I called in a felony stop and requested backup. Just then the suspect abruptly pulled over to the side of the road.

I pulled in behind and exited my vehicle with my gun drawn. I used my door for protection as I loudly shouted out, "Stay in your vehicle with your hands palm-forward on the inside of the windshield!" At that moment the driver, a white male approximately twenty-five years old with short brown hair, bolted from the car, and with his hands in his pockets he started walking towards me.

I was a trained professional ready for any situation that I might face, but this time I had to make a life-or-death decision. I could neither straddle the line and ponder the "what ifs" nor go back once a decision was made—this was it. My definite major purpose had been clearly defined: protect, serve, and stay alive.

As he continued to approach me, I yelled out, "Slowly take your hands out of your pockets or I will shoot." He laughed and continued walking towards me. As I assessed the situation, I made a decision and I told him directly and with complete conviction that on the count of two if his hands were not empty and above his head, I would shoot him. I proceeded with the count and as I was about to say two, the suspect pulled his empty hands from his pockets and raised them above his head. Would I have shot him? You bet. I knew what my primary purpose was, I made a decision, and I was ready to act if necessary.

As it turned out, even though he fit the description, he wasn't the robbery suspect—he was just a drunk who'd nearly gotten himself killed. He made a very wise choice to do as commanded because his life was in his own hands.

Have you heard this one before? "Well, we are getting married, and if it doesn't work out we will just get a divorce and move on." That is the loser's way of making a decision. Any couple who takes this approach is headed for failure. If we leave an avenue for escape, we can avoid the hard work it takes to make a relationship successful so we will end up taking advantage of our predetermined escape clause. Don't mishear me: some relationships need to end because of violence, dishonesty, etc. What I am talking about is a couple making the decision and doing everything in their control to make it work with a focus on the primary objective rather than on planning a retreat.

Some of us take a job and say, "If it doesn't work out, I will just quit." Again, this is not a decision a winner makes—this is one made by a person who is already planning an escape route, and thus it is doomed for failure. No matter what decisions we make, we must make them with conviction and passion. We must stop being wimps and looking for ways out. Let's get right into the center of life and take control of our destiny with a positive approach, not a failure mentality. Either stand up or don't.

When I have had issues with weight, alcohol, drugs, anger, marriage, work, or whatever, I have been able to deal with them, but first I had to make a firm decision. I have learned that successful, happy people make decisions about their lives and then take action. There is no room for retreat or the notion of quitting. They realize that failure is often the price of success, and unless there is a total and uncompromising commitment to the journey, they will not be successful. This doesn't mean that the means to the end may not change, or that there won't be many left and right turns, but the reverse gear has been removed from the equation.

One evening while on patrol, I responded to a residential fire. This was my first serious disaster situation. As I arrived on the scene, the house was fully engulfed in flames, and there were several injured adults and children in the street. I was the only unit on the scene at the time as neither my backup nor the fire department was yet present. I rolled up my window and did a call-in to describe the severity of the situation. As I evaluated the situation, I learned there might be a boy still in the house.

I ran towards the house and looked for a safe way in. The windows were exploding and the heat beat me to the ground. There was no way in or out, so I returned to the injured and tended to their needs until help arrived.

Once the fire was extinguished, we found a twelve-year-old boy dead on the second floor. As it turned out, there had been four other children in the room, and this twelve-year-old made the decision to help each of them out of the window to safety. The last boy he actually tossed out the window, which resulted in serious injury, but the boy was alive. However, the twelve-year-old was then overcome by smoke and was unable to save himself.

This young boy made a decision—a life-or-death one—and he died for his self-sacrifice. I made the decision not to enter the building, which I know was the right one, but it still haunts me to this day. I was twenty-one years old, and this was a night on which many life-changing decisions were made.

This was the graveyard shift so I arrived home at 9:00 AM, rattled to my very core. My hands were shaking and my heart was pounding. My wife was at work which meant I was alone with all my fears and conflicts. I had a decision to make at that moment: do I seek help with my feelings, or do I pop the top off a beer and drink myself to sleep? My decision at that moment launched me full steam ahead into my alcoholism. Up until that moment, I never drank normally as I did abuse it, but I always drank for the effect and the fun of it. Once I made the decision to drink to drown my anguish, life as I knew it changed forever.

By the age of twenty-six, I was totally bankrupt financially, physically, and spiritually. I was no longer a police officer. I had no job, and my wife was ready to leave me. I sat around the house in a bathrobe, forty pounds overweight, not groomed, drinking day in and day out. I could have remained suffering from the disease of alcoholism and self-centeredness, or I could make another life-altering decision to seek help.

One of these moments of awakening happened one summer evening in 1979 when Bonnie and I were at a party with her parents and some friends. As per my usual, I'd had several drinks and a few pills prior to the party, and continued drinking while there. As the evening progressed, I became more and more belligerent, obnoxious, and mean. I was sitting across the table from Bonnie, her parents, and friends when she said that I'd had too much to drink. This set me off and I took my drink and threw it all over her. She was embarrassed and humiliated.

I recall that moment as if it were yesterday. The look in her eyes, her body language, and the fear and the hopelessness sobered me up in an instant. I was full of shame, and I knew that I was out of control. I wish I could say that this moment sobered me up, but it didn't. There were many more moments such as this that had to occur until that final moment of conscious awareness (to be revealed later) that I had lost control of my life. Only then could I be ready for the path of a warrior.

Now that I have made that life-changing decision, my life has been a blessing and a blessing for those who love me. I have been able to teach thousands of people of all ages, including helping hundreds of drunks to get and stay sober. I have gained freedom from bondage and found peace in a new freedom.

If, however, I had decided to stay in my dead-end job, live in an unhappy marriage, or stay in other situations that were not the way of a warrior, I would still be miserable today. If I'd decided to remain in a situation that made me unhappy and unfulfilled, it would be my fault, and I would have forfeited my right to complain.

For example—if I am always complaining about my spouse's negative and unhealthy behaviors, and I have tried everything in my power to correct the situation to no avail, but I still stay in the relationship, then a decision has been made. I must then accept my decision in life and stop whining about it. I used to stew in my pain and misery and invite everyone around to suffer along with me. I didn't realize I was making a choice, and I should live with it or change it.

One night at an AA meeting, one guy as usual was complaining about his wife and her poor and resentful attitude. For months he'd been complaining about her, and the story was always the same. This particular evening, Paul, who was one of our members, spoke up with harsh words and said in a thoughtful tone: "Lou, either accept your spouse as she is or divorce her. We're sick and tired of hearing you whine and complain about a situation you do have control over. You either accept, love, and cherish her for all her defects and assets, or you divorce her."

Paul was so right, and he impacted my life with his teaching and his wisdom. Now I am able to recognize when I am whining and complaining about something over which I have control, but have made the decision to stick with the status quo. Today I take responsibility, and I don't create pity parties.

Can it be this simple? What if it is?

Think of some of our nation's greatest achievements, all of which began with someone having a purpose and a clearly defined goal, then making a decision with complete resolve. Martin Luther King, Jr.'s life's purpose was to expand the cause for equality. President Reagan's purpose was to see communism fall in the Soviet Union. President Kennedy decided we would put a man on the moon by the end of the decade. There are many more examples. The common thread to success stories and great achievements is that someone with a purpose makes a decision without building in an escape clause.

Were there failures along the way? Most certainly! But these people's resolve, purpose, and passion weren't crushed by failure or by all the dream busters who constantly tell us something can't be done. These people are no different than you or I—they have merely followed the steps that are being revealed to you now.

Let's now move on to the next step in our transformation and our unleashing of our inner warrior!

Chapter 6

Change Is a Gift

I would hear the word *change* and immediately cover my eyes and say something like, "Oh no! I can't handle change," or "I'm afraid of change." In fact, the only constant in life *is* change. The very thing that keeps life interesting and challenging is change.

My attitude and self-talk about change had to change. ("Oh no! Not change.") Yes, change. Instead of dreading and fearing change, I now embrace it, I look forward to it, and I invite it. I know the only way I will grow to my next level is by changing.

My father-in-law, Leo, is one of my true heroes. He demonstrated to me the meaning of willingness to change. He was a successful engineer working for Rockwell during the Apollo mission that put the first man on the moon. He had been an engineer his entire adult life until 1970 when he and several thousand employees at Rockwell were laid off. Suddenly, his whole world changed, and he had to change, too. Oh no, that *change* word again.

Leo had a stay-at-home wife (Shirley), three small children (Russell, Bonnie, and David), and a mortgage. You must understand that Leo was the clear definition of an anal retentive person. Don't hear this as a negative—for an engineer working in the space program, it was a good quality to have. But he was not a "people person," or at least that's what he thought. Out of necessity, Shirley went to work to help make ends meet while Leo searched for a new career.

Believe it or not, he eventually ended up in the insurance industry working with families, business men and women, companies and such. An engineer and an anal retentive man with little people skills who was stubborn as a mule was now a salesman.

This change, forced or not, turned out to be the best thing that ever happened to him and his family. By being willing to change, learn, and believe in himself, Leo found himself carrying out his true purpose in life. He grew a successful insurance business with thousands of clients. He softened his stubborn streak and learned that being of service to others was his passion.

He is one of my heroes, but not because he did anything extraordinary. He is my hero because he taught me that change is not a bad thing—it is merely a fact of life. I have a choice to embrace the change and focus on the journey, or I can freeze up, panic, and do nothing. He changed his life with grace and integrity, and that is a remarkable accomplishment.

You may be asking, "How much did you have to change?" My answer: pretty much everything. Exchange all negative thoughts with positive ones; exchange all negative, self-destructive actions with positive, successful ones. For me this meant I had to make a complete 180-degree transformation creating new habits with new and exciting patterns of thought and actions. I used to believe that I couldn't "change my mind." I know better now—I *can* change my mind once I have decided to do so and then take the appropriate action of a warrior.

I found that what is unknown challenged my confidence and my resolve, but then I learned that change is the seed for my growth and success. We plant the seed in the soil with the faith that it will grow into something beautiful. As the seedling is nourished, over time it begins to change and to grow. It is the same thing with change in our own lives. We plant a seed of an idea, a purpose, a direction, and we set out with faith. Soon the seed will show its true blessing and intentions. I had to be willing to walk through the door of change.

I had spent many of my years on this earth wanting what I wanted with no regard to the signs along the way. What I mean is this: I go along my way, thinking I know what is best for me and for my life, when all of a sudden I hit the obstacle—let's call it the wall. I know that beyond that wall is exactly what I want and need to make my life whole. It could be a certain kind of car, stereo, woman, clothing, etc. Whatever it may be, I am convinced that this thing is the answer to my dull and boring existence on this planet.

But here is the wall, and I don't know how to climb over it to get to the other side, so I back up to get a running start, take a deep breath, and plow into the wall head first. I do this over and over again until, bloody and beaten, I finally reach the other side. Each and every time I've done this, the results have been the same: the thing that I "knew" I needed negatively impacted my life. I refused to see the obvious sign—the wall itself.

One key to making life simpler is that if you hit the wall, turn left. In other words, don't fight the change—go with it. Of course, with my keen mind I analyzed this notion and asked my mentor, "What if I was supposed to turn right at the wall and not left?" He simply said that if that was the case, I would hit up against another wall, and I should turn left again. Then if I hit another wall, I should turn left. Eventually, I would end up on the right side! In doing so, I would save myself from the pain and futility of pounding down the wall. Turning left would allow my path to become the way I was supposed to be headed. The signs along our journey such as the wall are there for us to see and act on; otherwise we remain blind with a lack of purpose and vision.

When Bonnie and I were dating years ago, I was a very passionate and affectionate guy. Of course I was young and full of hormonal desires ... call me lustful! However, once we married and I turned to other aspects of my life, I became less affectionate and attentive to Bonnie's need for physical touch. I was always saying, "Well, I am just not an affectionate guy." We had gone to marriage therapists several times over the years, always over this same issue. We kept hitting the wall without turning left.

Here was our wall: I wanted and needed intimacy via sex, and Bonnie wanted sex via intimacy. I argued year in and year out that if she would give me what I wanted (sex), I would give her what she wanted (intimacy). I continued to be stubborn and refused to turn left and see the true path of the warrior. I wanted what I wanted and that was that.

In 2000 we went to yet another therapist to discuss this same issue. We were both bloody and exhausted from pounding our heads against the wall. One day I left work early in the day full of anxiety and frustration. I went home and took a nap, but before closing my eyes, I prayed for guidance. I said I was willing to turn left.

When I awoke thirty minutes later, I had the answer. I had spent my life wanting for myself and trying to change my wife into what I thought she should be. I was thinking about my own needs and desires, not the needs of the person I loved most in this world. Essentially I was demanding that she change to fulfill my needs. It was one of those moments of clarity: the signs had been there for decades, but I'd refused to see the answer. Instead I'd continued to exercise my own will rather than abide by the principles of a warrior.

From that moment on, I have spent my life trying to fulfill the needs of my wife. I am affectionate with her because it's what makes her happy, and even if it is difficult for me to do so, I know it is the way of the warrior. I have discovered that by fulfilling Bonnie's needs, my needs have also been met with open arms and with passion. The issue we had had for thirty-plus years simply disappeared one afternoon when I decided to turn left.

Insanity has been defined as doing the same thing over and over again expecting a different result. Think of that the next time you insist on tackling a wall of a problem by running into it over and over. Instead of hitting the wall demanding that your needs will be met, look for the open doors of opportunity. Sometimes by turning left, you can find your way through an open door.

In 1999, Alex, one of my black belts, approached me with a unique business opportunity. He was excited and motivated, but I resisted because I was viewing the opportunity in terms of concepts. I kept thinking of it as being similar to a pyramid scheme—something I wanted to avoid as I knew how people used them to take advantage of friends and family. However, I also knew that as a teacher, I was supposed to be willing to open an ear and at least listen. As skeptical as I was, I opened my mind.

I began to hear the truth rather than my misconceived perceptions. I began to understand that the business world had changed, but I was still living in the 1950s. My mind began changing because I was willing to be teachable. As Alex went on a mile a minute, he got me caught up in the excitement of the dream.

As my attitude began to change, so did my vision; and then my dreams expanded. I got into a networking online business whose foundation has been around for over fifty years. It is a plan for success based on principles and the warrior spirit of "one who serves." Alex opened this door of opportunity to my wife and me, yet I almost missed it because of my initial unwillingness to change.

Please know I'm not trying to sell you on a particular business. What I am talking about is my being open and willing to see that the business world has changed and continues to evolve. This change is nothing to fear, but something to embrace. Our business and its leadership, mentoring, and teaching program is growing and expanding every day. My wife has been able to retire from her job, and the additional income has allowed us the freedom from worry and given us the time and finances to do the things we love. Most important has been the blessings of helping so many others achieve their personal and financial goals. We are so glad we walked through that door and were willing to change.

My point is simple: unless we are willing to listen, learn, and change, we will miss the open doors of opportunity and continue to stay in our ruts. The only difference between a rut and a grave is the depth. I changed and decided to take action to climb out of the rat race and up to the next level. Up, up, and away!

Chapter 7

We Have to Plan or We Will Surely Fail

How many excuses can I conjure up? I know that I have used more excuses over my lifetime than I can count. Looking back, I can see they were nothing more than expressions of my unwillingness to do whatever it took, no matter what.

Let's talk about planning. Winston Churchill once reportedly complained, "One must always look ahead, but it is difficult to look farther than one can see." It's only when we have a purpose for tomorrow that today has substance. This is true about both the future of a company and the direction of an individual's life.

Planning is critical to using time effectively, because it bridges the gap between where we are now and where we hope to be at some future point. Think of it as a chasm. One side represents now, and the other side represents our objectives. Unless there's some way to bridge this separation, we'll never be able to achieve our goals.

I've always been a planner, and even through the major distractions of my life, having a plan has been critical to my success. When Bonnie and I married at ages eighteen and nineteen respectively, we had a plan: we planned to have two children (one girl and one boy), but we would wait for ten years to begin this family. Our plan was precise and agreed upon. During these ten years prior to having children, we planned to acquire a home; pursue careers; obtain insurance, transportation, and money in the bank; achieve stability in our marriage; and travel as a couple. Even with all our distractions, we managed to carry out our plan.

Time—there's never enough of it! I used to tackle urgent matters before important ones. Urgent matters are easy to identify, and are usually quicker and easier to do. Planning is one of those important matters that we put off until all urgent items have been taken care of. The problem is, when we constantly focus on the urgent instead of the important, we can find ourselves in a crisis that requires an immediate response, taking even more time away from our objectives and purpose. Many times this crisis might have been avoided through planning.

Some of us prefer to be doing, moving, and deciding. This leads us to adopt a reactive pattern of behavior. We react to whatever happens around us, often quite successfully. Planning is a proactive activity, but it doesn't provide much of the excitement of being in the thick of things.

Many of us like to gain a sense of closure from our tasks. We're often looking for rapid feedback, and planning doesn't provide it. We may not see the results of our plans for weeks, months, or sometimes years. With no immediate reward or reinforcement, planning may seem less interesting, and we create excuses not to do it.

In addition, many of us pride ourselves on our spontaneity and our ability to go with the moment. We view careful planning as a contradiction. We may feel that if we spend time planning, we'll miss the important things. This is not true. Our lives and our jobs are too complex to simply wing it all the time. If we want things to happen in the right way, we must plan. The better we plan, the more time we'll have for taking advantage of opportunities as the doors open for us.

Here are six effective ways of planning:

1. Clearly identify the root of the challenge or situation. Before jumping straight into the how-to-solve phase, be sure the underlying issue or situation has been completely identified.
2. Determine the objective you are trying to meet. Ask yourself how you will measure the success of the plan, and identify the logical checkpoints at which you can measure your progress.

3. Identify the specific activities necessary to reach your objectives. After establishing those activities, put them in priority order and attach time frames to each of those tasks. Consider staffing needs, costs, time, and available resources.

4. Realize that just because you took time to plan doesn't automatically mean you are ultimately going to carry out that plan. Only after you have completed the first steps will you have enough information to decide whether to move forward. Often you will find that decision is no. Does that mean the time you spent on the plan was wasted? Not at all. It is important to make go/no decisions based on rational criteria, which is what a good plan provides.

5. Set a finish date for the overall project so you know when it will be completed. Even if you've established time lines for individual tasks, it's important to set a final deadline.

6. Recognize that a follow-up phase is good for evaluating the plan. Ask yourself: How effective was the plan? Did the plan work? What could be improved next time? What did I learn from this process? During this step you may also want to wrap up final details and issue a final report.

Why do most people fail to achieve their true potential?

1. They are trapped in their comfort zones.
2. They have poorly constructed goals, causing procrastination.
3. They have poorly constructed action plans, causing confusion and wasting precious time.

The comfort zone is the area of the known, the safe, and the familiar in our lives. When we need to feel safe, we retreat to this zone, only to be drawn out of it by curiosity, self-confidence, or a sense of adventure. We must ask ourselves: when was the last time we stepped out of our comfort zone? Are we planning to step out again? How? Comfort zones grow and shrink with our self-confidence and sense of security. We must plan to step out and win, or we will surely fail!

Here are tips for planning and managing our time:

1. Recognize subconscious patterns that affect our lives.
2. Turn dreams, intentions, and desires into firm, achievable goals.
3. Overcome procrastination.
4. Conquer interruptions and time wasters.
5. Turn unproductive activities into productive ones.
6. Avoid the pitfalls of busywork.
7. Delegate more effectively.
8. Plan and prioritize each day.
9. Handle paperwork quickly.
10. Reduce stress and increase quality time.

Let's ask ourselves: what are the benefits we will receive by managing our time better? If we could add an extra hour or two to our day, what would we do with that time?

For many of us, balancing busy personal and professional lives is a major challenge. Trying to keep up with current changes in technology, changing expectations, career demands, and personal obligations is harder and harder. If we feel overwhelmed by our responsibilities, managing time well is the most important step we can take.

Here are some typical time wasters:

1. Lacking confidence in the facts
2. Insisting on having all possible facts
3. Fearing the consequences (either failure or success)
4. Lacking rational decision making
5. Failing to see the benefits of planning
6. Lacking priorities
7. Having broad interests
8. Being impatient with details
9. Responding only to the urgent
10. Attempting too much in too little time
11. Lacking planning

Look at all these time wasters. We are all guilty of some, if not all of them. Review your time wasters and make the necessary changes to free up time and energy for your passion and purpose in life. The information in this book is giving you the solutions. All you must do is take positive and directed action *one step at a time.*

The way in which we manage and plan time is often based on habit. We do what we do because we have always done it that way. Habits can get in the way when our situation, environment, or other factors change. Habits are unconscious behaviors that are automatic. Changing old habits can help us manage and plan time more effectively. The first step to making a change is to identify which habit patterns are beneficial and which are detrimental.

In his *The Principles of Psychology* (1890), American psychologist and philosopher William James suggests an approach to changing habits that is quite effective. In essence, he recommends that we:

1. Launch the new behavior as strongly as possible,
2. Seize the first opportunity to act on the new behavior,
3. Never let an exception occur until the new behavior is firmly rooted.

Dr Maxwell Maltz, a twentieth century cosmetic surgeon who studied the behavior changes of his patients after surgery, further suggested that simple habits can be broken and new habits put in place in about twenty-one days (*Psycho-Cybernetics*, 1960). Changing habits takes time and energy. Change is not easy, so you have to work on it.

Here are some tips for changing habits:

1. Remember, desire is the key to success or failure.
2. Be diligent, especially in the first four weeks.
3. Do not deviate from your new behavior. These new behaviors must be firmly rooted and become a new habit force.
4. Beware of crisis. When a crisis hits, you are likely to swing into action automatically, reacting in the ways you know best. Once in a crisis, your attention is on the immediate problem, not on

your new routine. You may push everything else aside and lapse into the old behavior.

So, beware of the things that trigger or cue your habit behaviors. Most behavior is a response to a stimulus, such as feeling hunger at the sight of tempting food, feeling anxiety after injuring yourself or receiving a bill in the mail, or feeling sadness over the death of a loved one. Recognize the triggers to behaviors you need to change. Once you identify the trigger events, you have three ways to approach them:

1. You can change the trigger event.
2. You can change your response to the trigger event.
3. You can change both.

Remember, no change will take place without desire, determination, and action.

Setting priorities is the act of assigning weight to a list of items. It is determining what is more important than something else. When setting priorities, a simple A, B, and C system works well:

a) "A" priority is anything that you *must* do as the task is critical to the successful performance of that situation or goal. Priority "A" needs to be taken care of fairly quickly or the consequences will be severe.

b) "B" priority is something you *should* do. It's also critical to successful performance because it has high value, but it's not as urgent as an "A" priority. If necessary, a priority "B" task can be temporarily postponed.

c) "C" priority is something that's *nice to do*. It is desirable to complete a priority "C" item, but it's not critical to the overall success of your objective. Priority "C" is often urgent, but rarely important. Examples include cleaning out the garage, putting together a scrapbook from a family vacation, or washing the windows.

Now, decide to prioritize your tasks. Use these questions to help you make your priority decisions:

> ➤ Why am I doing it?
> ➤ How does this relate to my goals/objectives?
> ➤ What is the immediacy of the task (i.e., how urgent is it)?
> ➤ Is it really important?
> ➤ Can anyone else do it?
> ➤ Does it bring me closer to, or further away, from my objective?
>   If the activity is not bringing me *closer* to my goal, then it stands
>   to reason I will be further away if I do it, because I am taking
>   time away from those activities that aid my progress.

Plan for the high-payoff activities. High-payoff activities are those that will provide the greatest benefit to you and your purpose. Low-payoff activities will not provide much payoff in either the short or long run. Dealing with high-payoff activities is often difficult because they are frequently large, complex, or time-consuming tasks. Many of these high-payoff activities get put on the back burner for less difficult tasks, which usually leads to a low payoff. For instance, my wife and I are in the process of helping our son, Jason, purchase a condominium. The high-payoff activities surrounding this event include securing a good location, good financing rate, insurance for the home, and so on. While it would be much easier to engage in a low-payoff activity such as buying furniture for the condo, the high-payoff activity is ultimately what will put a roof over Jason's head—and a good one at that.

Here are some simple ways to deal with high-payoff activities:

1. Schedule your day around high-payoff activities.
2. Divide the projects into bite-size pieces.
3. Set deadlines.
4. Stay focused.

Here is how to deal with low-payoff activities:

1. Delegate them if possible.
2. Systemize them.
3. Lower your standards.

4. Group them together.
5. Use shortcuts.

Identify your purpose in life—feel it, hear it, taste it, see it, and believe in it. Make a decision and plan for success. Remember: even Dorothy in *The Wizard of Oz* had a road map!

Chapter 8

Go to School, Get Good Grades, Get a Job?—
You Must Be Joking!

Life is like a game of cards. The hand that is dealt you represents determinism; the way you play it is free will.

Jawaharal Nehru

At the age of twenty-one, I was sworn in as a police officer in the city we resided in. I was convinced that this would be my lifetime career and that one day I would retire into the sunset. After all, I'd dreamed about this moment since I was six years old. I completed the police academy at the top of the list and won the award for being the most physically fit. The income was good and left us comfortable especially as Bonnie and I had no children at the time.

Bonnie and I bought a home in the hills and had a shiny new sports car. Life was good and our future was set. I'd done as I was told, get a college degree and get a job, so all was supposed to be well. Unfortunately, life throws us challenges disguised in many ways. How would we be able to predict that I would be medically retired from the police department at age twenty-six?

The nature of the events surrounding my retirement is a topic worthy of another book, but suffice it to say that the physical, mental, and emotional toll of being a police officer had left me battered, broken, and overweight—a mere shadow of the fit, enthusiastic officer I had been five years prior. I was drinking alcoholically and abusing numerous pain medications and antidepressants. I had gained forty pounds, and my back and neck were severely immobilized from numerous automobile accidents. Now I was twenty-six with a wife and a mortgage, but no job. Needless to say Bonnie and I were devastated, full of fear, and losing hope. Now what were we going to do? Our plans for the future and our stability were shaken to the very core.

This is what I'd been told: "The road to success is assured if you go to school, study hard, get good grades, go to college, get a degree, then get a job and work hard for thirty to forty years. At retirement, you can collect your retirement funds and Social Security, and you are set for life."

Here is the truth that I found out the hard way: "Go to school, get good grades, and get a job" is no longer the road to success and financial freedom. Very few companies and organizations have a long-term plan for their employees. Downsizing and outsourcing is the future. The days of old are gone. Retirement plans are failing, and Social Security is not a plan for security. And what about a personal tragedy such as I experienced?

The best way to prepare for life is to begin to live.
Elbert Hubbard

Many of us have a job and work long, hard hours. There is no shortage of hard-working men and women. But this is a not a plan for financial success in the twenty-first century. Today you can do the college deal, get a job, work hard for decades and retire, but you will have spent the majority of your life working for someone else's dreams, not fulfilling your own inherent purpose or acquiring any substantial amount of wealth to see you comfortably through retirement. Many of us will spend the most valuable elements of our life (i.e. youth, relationships, family, opportunities to travel, and time) working, and for what? Drive up to your local hamburger outlet, "big box" store, or market for groceries and notice how many "retired" individuals have to work merely to survive in their golden years.

Here is a fact: most of the wealthy in our country today are not formally highly educated people. Instead they are people with big dreams and a purpose—people who are highly motivated and driven to succeed. They are not any smarter than you and I; they have simply stepped away from the masses and created a Plan B. They recognized that Plan A is a plan for mediocrity and commonality, not for financial freedom.

Don't misunderstand me. You may be the one who is highly educated and motivated, someone who has a plan. You may be making all the money you want and have all the free time you desire. If this is your story, then my hat's off to you. Unfortunately, that is not the story of the masses.

In our online network business, we come across hundreds of adults, both single and married, and it is quite a challenge to help them. Most of these people are not happy; they work hard for long hours with little time to enjoy their families or life in general. They want something else as in fact, they are bankrupt in most areas of their lives.

The frustrating thing is that success is not for those of us who need it or for those of us who want it—it is for those of us who work smart for it. We all have twenty-four hours in a day. We all have life challenges, ups and downs, good and bad times. Why is it that some of us reach success and some don't?

Those of us who are climbing to the top of the ladder are doing it by taking the first step and then continuing on the journey via the principles I am sharing in this book. We weren't lucky or smarter than you—we just followed the path of those successful people who came before us.

I look eye to eye with these folks we come across in our business and see their fear and their desperation. The problem is that many are not ready or willing to change and act in a way that requires stepping out of their comfort zones. Why would I rather watch television than go out and achieve great and positive things? I was comfortable being uncomfortable. How sad is that?

We started our online networking business with the *belief* that it would work. Now after several successful years working within the system of teaching and education, we have come to the point of *knowing* it. I say "we" because my wife was a huge part of making this happen. We were both willing to step out of our comfort zone and make the changes necessary to make our business work and work well. It has freed up time to spend with family, friends, hobbies, and charities.

Remember I said that I didn't have to change much, just everything! This doesn't mean I had to go out and quit my job, get a divorce, or move to another county. What I am saying is that I had to be willing to open my mind, let go of old ideas, identify bad habits, find my purpose, make a plan, find a mentor, and follow the steps. This takes changing, this takes faith, and this takes a decision.

I had to ask myself, am I living with a 1950s mentality, or will I resolve myself to live fully in the new world? Yes, doors of the past are being closed, but new and exciting doors to success are opening and available to those of us willing to step forward. All it takes is a "warrior" mentality and spirit!

One way to get the most out of life is to look upon it as an adventure.

William Feather

Chapter 9

Sweet Surrender

Lying in bed at age twenty-five, drunk, loaded on pills, and passed out, the educated law enforcement officer with all those lofty dreams and hopes was now nothing more than a pitiful, incomprehensible loser. As I lay there, I noticed my body was paralyzed. I literally could not move my body or talk. I could see myself in bed as if I were looking down at myself. I watched as my wife Bonnie shook me and called to me while tears ran down her face. Eventually I woke up and did it all over again, day after day.

I was drinking and abusing pain killers to the point of near death. Thank God, we didn't have children at this time, as Bonnie was carrying all the burdens of the world on her shoulders. She tells me today that she could see the man inside the drunk, she had faith in my resolve, and she believed I would have an awakening and turn my life around. She would have been well within her rights to turn tail and run, yet she persevered and she believed.

I know now what I did not understand back then: that I was full of fear and self-doubt. I was scared to live and equally scared to die. I felt like a failure, and I believed that my life was doomed for a disastrous end. "What's wrong?" everyone asked. "Why are you doing this to yourself? Why don't you stop?" At that point in my disease, I needed a spiritual awakening—not a flash of lightning, but help from a power greater than myself.

For the first time in my life I truly asked for help: help from anyone, anything, any way. I decided I couldn't do life by myself and that I needed to seek out guidance and instruction. As my old ideas had gotten me to where I was, I realized other people might know a better way. This is the point in my life that I came into contact with the support group of Alcoholics Anonymous. There, I was introduced to a set of principles—steps for living life on life's terms.

Equally important, I reached out for help. I received help from the fellowship and from my newly defined loving God. I was no longer in charge of the world. I was freely given a plan of action that gave me not only the choice to stay clean and sober, but a chance to live life beyond my wildest dreams.

I began to rely on the help of others who had gone before me. I was able to share my fears and my shortcomings and build a new and improved foundation for living. I had to change everything, and I was ready to meet the challenge with humility and enthusiasm.

As time went on and my life in sobriety began to improve, I noticed a change in all aspects of my life. My relationship with Bonnie was happy once again. I was back at work and planning to live my life one day at a time with purpose.

It has not all been a bed of roses, but I have been taught that I can choose to focus on the thorns of the rose or on the beauty as it blossoms. Today, I focus on the solutions, not the problems.

What turned me around was my willingness to surrender and to accept the fact that I am human. As an individual, my power is limited, but as part of a team, as a student, and as a teacher working towards a common goal and purpose, there is power. Alone, I will fail—together we will win. This required me to learn humility, to let go of ego, and to be willing to be vulnerable.

Successful people always surround themselves with people smarter than themselves—a team excited about the dream, pulling in the same direction. I have mentors for several aspects of my life. I have a person who mentors me in AA, with others for my marriage, for being a father, and for my career and karate. The mentors help me with financial, spiritual, and motivational matters. I am always looking for someone who is ahead of me and has something I want, then I seek out that person's advice and teaching.

Today I mentor others as much as I am mentored, as this is the process. I can't keep what I don't give away. You must also be willing to seek out mentorship and guidance, but this requires definite action. Look to those who are achieving their life goals and have something similar to what you want, then ask them to mentor you. Open your mind and ears and close your mouth. Listen and learn—this way you can grow to your next level and avoid making the same mistakes they already have made.

How important is mentorship? From my experience and my research, it is a *must*. Seek out the winners in life, follow their path, and when you fall, get back up and seek more advice and guidance.

It was time to stop saying, "I'll do it myself"—that sounds like a little child with self-will run riot. Nothing of great value will be achieved without team spirit and without our ability to be taught and then to teach. We must depend on one another the way the animals depend on trees for shade and fish depend on water to survive.

I have learned to surrender to my lack of power; and once I did surrender and follow a few simple steps, I gained more power and more control over my life and my destiny. My inner warrior was freed to be of service and to prosper.

I don't drink or use drugs, and I haven't for a very long time. I no longer wanted to look down from the ceiling at myself in a helpless, powerless, and disgraceful state, as this was not how I wished to be remembered. I decided I needed help, and that very decision has allowed me a life of dreams coming true and blessings for which I am so grateful.

Today the men and women in my life who are my mentors reach out to me, and I reach out to them. We each are responsible and accountable. We are honest and we are principled. But most of all, we are helping one another to become the best we can be and to achieve our dreams and purpose in life. You are free to do it all by yourself—it is your choice—but trust me when I say, "Surrender and seek guidance and mentorship." This is the easier, softer, and smarter way to achieve your dreams and your purpose!

None are more hopelessly enslaved
than those who falsely believe they are free.

Johann Wolfgang von Goethe

Chapter 10
The Extra Mile with Attitude

I am a firm believer that going the extra mile is mandatory in all areas of my life. I've discovered that very few people are willing to do what it takes to get to their next higher level because they don't understand the value of the extra mile.

Let me give you a couple of examples that have helped me understand the way of the warrior. I opened the doors to my first martial arts studio in 1992. One of my first students was a twelve-year-old named Caleb. Rhonda, his mother, brought him into my office asking for help. Caleb was a chubby boy with apparently no athletic abilities. His father and brothers were jocks, but Caleb never fit in with any sport he attempted. Rhonda asked if we would be able to help him connect.

I was immediately moved by her appeal. Rhonda had a desire in her heart that was passionate and motivating, and I wanted to be of service. I enrolled Caleb on the spot, and he attended his first class an hour later.

From the very start, Caleb was excited and enthusiastic. He indicated to me that he loved his first lesson, and he felt as if he had found something he could truly enjoy. In fact, from that point on, Caleb was my shadow. He was curious about everything—and I mean everything. He would do all the little things. He was always present and available to help out, run errands, clean toilets, empty trash, and study extra materials. He did these things with a zest and passion that was surpassed only by my passion. He was excited and he was full of purpose—smiling, laughing, working, learning and dreaming.

As our studio grew in numbers, Caleb's role increased, and with that, so did his desire and passion to be of service. It wasn't long after that first class that Caleb's parents approached me and said that he was a changed young man. He was excited about life, and he seemed happy.

I explained to them that Caleb had found a purpose in his life and a reason to get up in the morning. He had set his plan in motion through his attitude and his going the extra mile. Caleb grew up with our studio, shadowing me day after day, week after week, and year after year. He was learning how to teach, how to connect to people, and how to run a business.

Unfortunately, Caleb was not doing well in high school, and was in jeopardy of falling into the wrong crowd. He also was dabbling with alcohol and very easily could have spun out of control. We were all very concerned.

Rhonda and I took a walk in the park one afternoon, and she asked for my opinion and help. I told her Caleb was a fine young man with a definite major purpose. His dreams were well-defined, and martial arts was his passion in life. I suggested Caleb come live with me and my family for a short while. Caleb would work with me, train with me, and learn many things he would need to become successful and happy. During that time he could take the equivalency test so as to graduate early from high school.

Rhonda and Brian, Caleb's dad, love him beyond belief; and with love they agreed so our plan was set into motion. Caleb was so excited and happy. For the next few years, even after he returned home, we worked side by side at the karate academy. He attended business conventions and AA meetings with me, and he got involved in his church. We went through many challenges, but we helped Caleb stay focused on his purpose, and the results tell the story.

Today, Caleb is twenty-seven and an associate here at our karate academy. He is married to Kim and has two daughters and a son. He is an assistant pastor at his church and a chaplain for a local police department. In part due to his work at our studio, he currently earns a yearly income of well into six figures and still has the same passion and enthusiasm with complete clarity of his purpose in life. He is a warrior.

This is a prime example of someone going the extra mile physically and emotionally, with a great attitude and with a purpose.

Bonnie is another great example of attitude and going the extra mile. We married in 1973 when we were very young. At eighteen, Bonnie had already completed one year at a local university and was excited about one day working with children. However, because of our financial situation, she had to withdraw from school and find employment. Knowing that her passion was working with people and especially children, Bonnie had a plan of action.

She approached her childhood dentist and offered the following: she told him she loved working with children, yet she knew nothing about the dental field. She suggested she come to work for him for six months at no pay. All she wanted in return was to apprentice and to prove her value. Bonnie said, "If you see value in my employment, you can then put me on the payroll, but if I show no promise, let me go."

Within a few weeks Bonnie not only proved to everyone at the dental office that she had a great attitude but that she was willing to go the extra mile. She showed up early, stayed late, and shadowed the doctor, staff, and even the cleaning crew. She studied and practiced on her own time and made it clear she was purpose driven. The children loved her. This turned into a twenty-five-year career.

The extra mile doesn't mean that we just show up early and stay late. It doesn't mean that we just do the "extras" around the office and at home. It's not enough that we're physically going through the motions of going the extra mile—there must be more.

It is remarkable how attitude and extra attention creates an environment for success. There are many truths in the world such as "we reap what we sow," "honesty is the best policy," and "do unto others as you wish them to do unto you." It is also a universal truth that what we put out into the universe—such as an attitude of gratitude—will be returned to us tenfold.

Attitude is the key. When we have a good and positive attitude, we will reap what we sow. If we have a bad attitude, again we will still reap what we sow. If we combine purpose, passion, excitement, enthusiasm, action, and going the extra mile, we can't help but succeed.

So, how did I develop a positive attitude? First and foremost I began to trust myself and my good instincts. I needed to learn that hardly any mistake or misfortune is the end of the world. As trite as it may sound, I began looking at the glass as half full rather than half empty. I have a *choice* every day about how I view the world. I look for the sunshine in the breaks of the clouds. I focus on the nice compliment someone gives me, and keep my distance from negative people who want to steal my sunshine.

I want to conclude this chapter with one of my favorite verses—this version is widely attributed to Mother Teresa and reportedly was inscribed on the wall of her home for children in Calcutta:

People are often unreasonable, illogical, and self-centered;
Forgive them anyway.
If you are kind, people may accuse you of selfish, ulterior motives;
Be kind anyway.
If you are successful, you will win some false friends and some true enemies;
Succeed anyway.
If you are honest and frank, people may cheat you;
Be honest and frank anyway.
What you spend years building, someone could destroy overnight;
Build anyway.
If you find serenity and happiness, they may be jealous;
Be happy anyway.
The good you do today, people will often forget tomorrow;
Do good anyway.

Give the world the best you have, and it may never be enough;
Give the world the best you've got anyway.
You see, in the final analysis, it is between you and your God;
It was never between you and them anyway.

Chapter 11

The Moments Count

Life is filled with so many exciting twists and turns. Hop off the straight and narrow whenever you can and take the winding paths. Experience the exhilaration of the view from the edge. Because the moments spent there, that take your breath away, Are what make you feel truly alive.

Stacey Charter

I have missed so many of the moments in my life, whether it was because of failure to pay attention, ignorance, being drunk, or being focused on the unimportant. When I got sober and began to turn my life around, I decided then and there not to waste another moment ever again.

There would be events in my past that I can't remember, things I was too busy to notice or too drunk to recall. I can look back at old photo albums and see that Bonnie and I were having a great time in some faraway exotic location, yet I can't remember the event or sometimes even being there.

What I regret most was missing the small moments—the moments that are so precious and so endearing. I am now known around AA meetings as the guy who always talks about the "moments." I say it is the moments, good and not so good, that keep me sober and alive each and every day. If at all possible, I don't want to miss those moments because they are the treasures I am harvesting. The moments become my blessings and my inspiration to go on.

When my daughter, Sheri, was in junior high school, she and a girlfriend worked long and hard on a video project for a school history contest. The winners would go on to city, county, and then state competitions. They put their heart and soul into a video that focused on the horrors of the Holocaust. The project was beautifully prepared and heart wrenching.

They got to the competition that would have brought them to the state competition. Their project was displayed and viewed on a Saturday, and we were all there expecting that they would win. In fact, all her teachers felt that their project was a lock and all of us were flying sky high. I had no doubt in my mind that they would win, but when the announcement was made for first place, their names weren't called, and all of our hearts dropped like a lead balloon. That was a moment I will never forget.

Sheri was in full tears mode. She was crushed, and so were we. That was one of those moments when I wished I could have controlled the results of the contest in my daughter's favor. I embraced her and consoled her and helped her through that moment with love and kindness. I could neither change the outcome nor the emotional letdown we all felt. Yet the moment turned into one of tears, hugs, and love. We made it past the moment and into acceptance. I look back at that moment with sadness at the results of the contest, but happiness as being a moment we bonded and shared our emotions as a family.

Sheri has given me so many moments—most of joy and pride, but some others full of drama. I'm so glad I was present for all of them. I mean actually *present*—mind, body, and spirit. I remember the night we were at the local theater watching Sheri perform in a play. I felt for a moment I was the only person in the audience and that I could see, hear, and feel my daughter up on stage as if it were in slow motion. I took that moment and firmly etched it into my heart. I felt so much love, pride, and joy. I knew that this was a moment of blessing, and I might have missed it.

I had another very powerful moment in 2006. At 2 AM our phone rang. Bonnie answered. I could hear Sheri screaming and crying over the phone, so I took it from Bonnie and asked Sheri to tell me what was going on. Apparently she had just finished up with a commercial acting job and was on her way home from Los Angeles when she got lost in a very rundown, seedy neighborhood. As she went through an intersection, she was broadsided by another vehicle. She was shocked as her car spun 180 degrees.

She made the decision to drive to a safer location and then phone for help. This was a moment when I was so grateful for my sobriety and my experience. I was able to guide Sheri to a safe location, then drive to her and help her. I was able to manage my fear and my emotions enough to be a father and to be a warrior. Sheri was amazingly composed and made very wise decisions at a very critical and dangerous moment in her life.

Two years ago Bonnie and I took a trip to the Grand Canyon with her mom and dad. It was wonderful. As I took a moment at the ridge of the canyon, I once again felt the moment come alive. I embraced it with all of my being, and it is etched on my memory for life. I could have missed it. There are so many moments that I just sit back and look at what life has to offer—all the blessings of sobriety, and my wife and children, family and friends, and freedom.

The world is beautiful when I take a moment to stop and actually be present. So many times I was there, but not "all there." I must experience all moments of the day rather than pay little or no attention to them. I used to do whatever I could to avoid emotional pain and reality. *The only problem with reality is that it is so real.* I drank, used drugs, overate, ran away, quit, and hid, all to avoid reality. Why is this? I had a loser mentality, which is the way of the wimp.

I was responsible for missing the moments, both good ones and not-so-good ones. Shame on me. Life is not a dress rehearsal. What was I waiting for?

I wasn't enjoying life—I was just passing the moments by until my death. I had nobody to blame but myself. But now I have found the passion and the value in the moments and embrace them. These moments are the fuel that generates greatness.

Greatness is not just in the reaching of our goals. It is priceless because of the moments along the way. All the wonderful things that

I experience today are not just in photo albums—they are burned into my heart and soul. Whether times are good or not, we must be present for the moment; otherwise we might as well be dead.

I stopped the merry-go-round of life in order to smell the roses. I embrace life on life's terms. I take negative distractions out of my life and replace them with all the good this life has to offer. I stopped pretending and now just accept the moment for what it is.

The gift of life is always in the present, yet so many of us are always projecting into tomorrow and beyond. What will be, will be, and what is, is. The gift of the present, like any other gift, is to be opened at that moment; that is why it is called "the present." I won't miss out on it by looking to what *might* be—I enjoy the present moments.

At the end of my day I take a moment and count my blessings. I find that the blessings all come in the form of moments, and I feel gratitude, joy, and peace in the present. After all, it is my gift if I choose to live it.

They say that any day above ground is a good one—maybe, in the sense that at least we're not dead. However, I've modified that slightly to say that any day above ground where I am present and in the moment, fulfilling my purpose and directing my energies toward what is good, is a good day.

I challenge myself every moment to, see, hear, feel, and experience. I meditate just for a moment and take time to actually feel it and embrace it for what it is, then embed it in my mind and heart. There are blessings in the moments that I must not miss.

One day at a time—this is enough. I refuse to look back and grieve over the past for it is gone, and I am not troubled about the future, for it has not yet come. I live in the present and make it so beautiful it will be worth remembering.

I recommend you to take care of the minutes,
for the hours will take care of themselves.

Lord Chesterfield

Chapter 12

Acting Our Way into Better Living

So many fail because they don't get started—they don't go.
They don't overcome inertia. They don't begin.

W. Clement Stone

Let me start this chapter by saying that many of us are taking some of the action required to achieve our dreams, vision, and purpose in life. We all must take a look inward and ask ourselves, "Am I taking directed action or not?"

We have all heard these words, "We can think our way into better living" or "We can think our way into financial freedom," or even better, "What we think, we will become." However, in and of itself, thinking our way into something isn't effective. If it were, no one would be overweight, poor, unhealthy, out of shape, living in a slum, or even on the street. In fact, I thought and told myself a thousand times that I wasn't going to get drunk—yet I always did.

The fact of the matter is that I was lazy and I was constantly complaining about what I didn't have—and what I wished I had—instead of taking the necessary action to make it so. How many times did I say, "I am going to diet so I look and feel better. I am going to exercise and get back into shape. I will be healthy, happy, wealthy, and wise!"

I said these things, somehow believing that as long as I thought the thoughts, they would come true. Then I'd start the complaining and whining all over again, making new promises, thinking about what was going to happen, and yet doing nothing again and again. I was a part of the society of complainers who don't want to hear, speak, or live in reality.

Television shows, books, magazines, lectures, and workshops generate billions of dollars a year getting us to believe we can get what we want by thinking about it; in the long run, however, it is only our actions that count. As long as we are willing to read the books, hear the message, and think about it, but take no action, we will continue to spend those billions of dollars so we can think our way into better living. Right—that is what the ones who sell these things are counting on. They know we won't *do* the things necessary to get the job done. We, as a society, have proven that decade after decade.

I couldn't *think* my way into better living—I had to *act* my way into better living. I refused to believe that although I'd had this notion for many years that I could think my way into accomplishing my goals and dreams, it had never worked. Now I know that as I'm not that talented, I can't succeed at anything if I don't take action. Those of us who are out of a job, in a job we hate, in an unhappy relationship, or in whatever situation we want to change might need to do something positive in the right direction—we need to take action!

In the earlier chapters I mentioned that at one point in my life, I was bankrupt in every area of my life—financially, physically, emotionally, and spiritually. I found the only way I could get from there to here (healthy) was to finally take positive action and not quit.

Nike has a slogan, "Just Do It"! Actions speak louder than words and thoughts. We will ultimately be judged on our actions, not our intentions.

I went into the AA program and asked for help. They gave me specific instructions. They said that AA is a program of action, and if I was willing to take direction and get off my butt and do it, I had a chance for recovery. So I did—and it worked. I examined my relationships, and instead of wishing and whining, I took action—and it worked. Instead of just showing up each and every day to my job, I took action and sought out mentors who could teach me how to become financially free—and it is working.

Take time to deliberate, but when the time for action has arrived,
stop thinking and go in.

Napoleon Bonaparte

Have you ever said or heard this one: "I tried that, but it didn't work for me"? Or, "Well, I tried AA, and it didn't work for me," or "I tried that diet and it didn't work for me"? Here is the truth: in order for anything to work, we must work for it, not it for us. A person can't come into AA and expect us to get and keep him or her sober—the person must work for it.

When I give a half-hearted effort at whatever I attempt, I may blame that "thing" for not working when in fact I haven't done what was necessary for success. Most of the time we quit before the miracle occurs. Some even quit after the miracle has occurred. Imagine that!

It is time for us all to stand and cheer for the doer, the achiever—the one
who recognizes the challenge and does something about it.

Vince Lombardi

In AA, in business, and in relationships, there are steps for success. They have been proven throughout the centuries to work. They are called *steps* for a reason. We are directed to take the steps in order to arrive at our target destination. Who will do it for me if I don't?

We are the home of the brave and the land of the free, but I think we, as Americans, need to remember that we must be brave enough to take full advantage of the freedom that has been granted us through the sacrifice of those who have come before us and those presently protecting our freedoms. We must stand and take action to leave this country and our world a better place when it is our time to go. We must stop expecting results unless we are willing to work for them.

How about these statements: "I have to find my true self" or "I need to learn to love myself"? These are two phrases I would like to have had deleted from my vocabulary. I was so interested in myself that I forgot that being of service is the way to fulfillment and inner happiness. I can't learn to love myself, and I won't find my true self unless I care about others. This is the way of the warrior.

I have found that when I am nice, when I am genuinely interested in others, and when I am being of service, I get out of "self." I don't believe we can learn to love ourselves or find our true selves when all we focus on is self. It is when we give to others, help others, and reach out to others that we can truly have something to love in ourselves. We gain confidence, inner strength, and inner peace, and eventually we find serenity and satisfaction in being a warrior as one who serves.

I had to go outside of my comfort zone and help someone in need, or listen to a friend rather than talk about myself. I had to be interested in my fellow human beings and search out what I can give rather than what I can receive or take. When I give of myself, I am able to conclude my day feeling significant and worthy of self-love.

You can't live a perfect day without doing something for someone who will never be able to repay you.

John Wooden

When I am having a bad day, I get out of self and do something of service for others. I go serve food at a shelter, answer a help line at a crisis center, or talk with the lonely at a hospital or retirement home. These are the actions of a warrior. I assure you that my troubles vanish when I'm not thinking about myself all the time.

For years I heard the phrase, "act as if," and I absolutely believe this to be true. How we act tells the story—it is about attitude and presentation. I've been conducting women's self-defense seminars since 1975, and one of the most important messages I have to get across is attitude and actions. When we walk, talk, and present ourselves as victims, we are more likely to become victims. Unless our very presence indicates confidence and self-awareness, we will be vulnerable to those who will take advantage of us.

It doesn't matter if you're having the worst day ever, you must hold your head up straight, with your shoulders upright and eyes confident and aware, and put on a smile rather than a frown. All of us can sense when someone is in a bad or a good mood. Confident or depressed— the key is to act as if you are having a great day and to be of service to others—in other words, get out of self. There is always someone having a worse moment than you.

My mentors have taught me this by their actions and their example. I have watched many of my men and women friends live and die with grace and dignity. My very good friend in AA who has been my mentor since 1984 is very ill with bone cancer. Of course I am very sad, but the other day when I asked him how he was (he looked terrible), he said, "I have learned to live with dignity and gratitude, and now I am learning to die with grace, dignity, and gratitude." He smiled and gave me a hug as we slowly walked into a meeting.

What he shared with the group that evening wasn't about himself, but how grateful he is that he has so many friends and family, and how he has become a man with pride and integrity: a man who will leave a lasting legacy of love. It wasn't about him—it was him giving to the group. He was not interested in what we could do for him—he wanted to be of service to us. This is a lesson for all of us.

I am determined to learn from my mentors and continue to *act* myself into better living!

Only those who have learned the power of sincere and selfless contribution
Experience life's deepest joy: true fulfillment.

Anthony Robbins

Chapter 13

IDEA

Whatever you vividly imagine, ardently desire, sincerely believe, and
enthusiastically act upon ... must inevitably come to pass!

Paul J. Meyer

I have shared at great length the importance of identifying our unique purpose in life. What is it that floats our boat? What is it that we should be doing that we aren't—and what are we doing that we shouldn't? If we are not living for something greater than self, then we have not yet found our purpose.

Purpose in and of itself creates an environment that feeds the fire within us. It creates energy and enthusiasm. The more we direct our energies toward the target, the more successful and happier we will be.

Here Is an IDEA That Has Served Me Well

Step 1—Identifying Our Purpose and Dreams in Life. I clearly identify what my dreams are, and *I dream big.* I see my dream clearly and get excited about the journey. We can accomplish whatever we desire if we uncover and discover our definite major purpose. This is critical! Seriously, grab a sheet of paper and start putting down what you find you get passionate about. Then continue reading ...

71

Step 2—Making a Decision. Once I have made my purpose and dreams clear in my heart and soul, it is time to make a decision. Once I make this decision, I step over the line of no return and move forward to the next step indicated. I stop thinking about it and do something that propels me forward, no matter how small the action might be.

There cannot be any *quit* in my mind. I dedicate myself to my intended target and don't let myself be distracted by life. I then begin to notice the doors opening, and I am directed toward my purpose—I step through the door with both feet.

We need to decide that we are worth having the very best that life has to offer. Decide that our past is the past and our future is in our hands. Decide to stop blaming people, places, and things for our situation and take responsibility for our life. Decide that we are warriors, ones who serve. Find out what we can do for others instead of what we can get from them. Decide that the buck stops here, and the decision has been made!

Step 3—Riding the Wave of Excitement and Enthusiasm. Once I have identified my purpose and have clearly stepped over the line and made a decision, I find myself full of excitement and energy—so much in fact that it is hard to sleep at night. My mind keeps racing with enthusiasm and new ideas for success. My energy and enthusiasm attract others, and more doors will open.

Our family, friends, and co-workers will notice this new attitude—one filled with purpose and expectation. We will appear happier and more successful, and our demeanor will attract success and happiness. Excitement breeds excitement, enthusiasm breeds enthusiasm, and winning breeds winners. Let's be winners! It is an energy pill far better than any drug we will ever take.

Step 4—Taking Action. With these three steps firmly embedded in our life, it is time to take action. We have uncovered a purpose and a direction. We have made the decision, gotten excited and enthusiastic—now we need to get moving. Action is the cornerstone to our success. Without action, the first three steps are mere hopes and wishes.

Action comes in many forms such as planning, researching, learning, and tapping into mentors. But it is the action involved in all these things that will continue to recharge our batteries and keep us directed and on course. As my mentor says, "Take the next appropriate action." If we are aware and alert, then that necessary action is usually right in front of us. Let's not miss out because we are distracted by life. We are *purpose* driven, not crisis driven!

To make it simple to incorporate into our life, IDEA is the way of the warrior:

I - **I**dentify your Purpose and Dreams in Life
D - Make a **D**ecision
E - Ride the Wave of **E**nthusiasm and Energy
A - Take **A**ction

Chapter 14

Personal Freedom

True individual freedom cannot exist without economic security.
Franklin Delano Roosevelt

I was born in the United States of America, a free country. As far back as I can remember, I've been told—not necessarily by my own parents, but by our society in general— that I am free to be whatever I hope to be and that all my dreams can come true. After all, we live in the land of opportunity. We can travel at will, eat whatever and wherever we please, work where we choose, go to school, and even vote in matters of national and local importance. The freedoms we have in America are too numerous to count.

In this chapter I wish to share with you what personal freedom means to me. Personal freedom is a matter of breaking out of the bondage of self. Even though we live in a free society, many of us are still enslaved by our own self-centered attitudes, habits, and comfort zones. Most of us take for granted the opportunities freedom provides.

Individual freedom is not free. We must first work for it before we can live it. It's not something handed to us on a silver platter. Why is it that so many immigrants to the United States take full advantage of our educational system and become successful? I contend that they appreciate individual freedom and understand that freedom is an opportunity, not a gift package.

In 1991, I seemed to have my life together. I was thirty-nine, married, and the father of two children. I had a home and money in the bank, and eight years of sobriety behind me. At the time I had been attending four AA meetings per week, working with my mentor, and helping other alcoholics. I was on top of the world. However, I allowed my ego to run rampant, and soon I stopped going to meetings and counseling sessions with my mentor. I turned my back on helping others and took credit for my success. I thought I was in control.

It wasn't long before I walked out of our home one day and went directly to the liquor store where I bought a bottle of vodka and toasted my "freedom." I was drunk from that point on until I hit a horrifying, shameful, and nearly disastrous bottom one year later. By the time my mentor found me and got me to the emergency room, I was nearly dead. In fact I was so near death that they were calling for a rabbi to come in and comfort me in my last remaining moments. I could have lost everything: my marriage, children, friends, career—and life itself.

What I learned was that personal freedom is something I earn each and every moment of my life. I can't rest on my laurels and allow my self-centered ego to take over. I have to want to live life to its fullest and practice good principles and morals in all areas.

I have had to work very hard to gain and maintain personal freedom from self-bondage. As a young man, I was full of self-centeredness and felt that the world owed me. I was imprisoned by my disease of alcoholism, fear, lack of confidence, and lack of faith. Had I not taken the necessary action, I would still be in my own personal prison. I had to come to appreciate freedom and want it so much that I was willing to take on my own demons.

First I had to admit that I was lazy, self-centered, selfish, and full of fear. I had to admit that I was an alcoholic; that I was powerless over people, places, and things; and that the only thing I have control over is me and my actions and my attitude. No one else is responsible for my behavior; and even though I didn't have a very good youth, I am responsible for the repairs. I have become a peaceful warrior!

Once I identified these facts, I had to decide to do something about it. I stepped over the line and decided right there and then that I was going to do whatever it took to become personally free from my own self-bondage. This was exciting and encouraging, and I was full of enthusiasm—at which point I was ready to take action.

Again, the IDEA factor was the key to freedom. Once I began to take positive action, I was on the road to recovery and freedom. I entered a twelve-step program to address alcoholism, I educated myself on business, relationships and how to deal with life on life's terms. I sought out mentors in all areas of my life.

I was teachable, humble, and willing to take direction and change. As I began to take hold of those things I had control over (self), I could feel the weight being lifted from my shoulders. As I learned that life was not all about me, I began to appreciate others for who they were. My fear was replaced with faith, and my confidence grew as I began to be of service to others.

My relationships improved dramatically merely by my giving more than I expected to receive. I began to see that God was doing for me what I couldn't do for myself. My fear of financial insecurity was lifted, and I gained a new peace. With time and willingness, I went from the believing to the knowing.

The average man does not want to be free.
He simply wants to be safe and independent.

H. L. Mencken

Let's talk about the meaning of the word *agnostic*: Merriam-Webster's defines it as "a person who holds the view that any ultimate reality (as God) is unknown and probably unknowable," or "a person unwilling to commit to an opinion about something." Most of us react from an agnostic viewpoint to anything and everything until we have enough experience, strength, and hope to move from the believing to the knowing.

I believed I loved Bonnie from the day we met on Halloween 1970. I believed this with all my heart back then, but today after more than 35 years of marriage, I *know* I love her and that she loves me. I believed I could become a police officer; in 1973 when I was sworn in, I went from the believing to the knowing. I believed I could get and stay sober, and after numerous years of sobriety, I went from the believing to the knowing. I believed I could find personal freedom—today I know it.

As a martial artist and a teacher, it is my responsibility and my privilege to help thousands of people to achieve personal freedom in body, mind, and spirit. As students progress through this process, it is a blessing to see them transition from the agnostic to the knowing. Through their willingness to be teachable, honest, and diligent, personal freedom has been earned and is now being lived.

The Serenity Prayer has been a huge help in my going from bondage into freedom:

God, grant me the serenity to accept the things I cannot change,
the courage to change the things I can and
the wisdom to know the difference.

I simply stopped putting my energy into trying to change those things in life that I have no control over such as people, places, and things. I accept the fact that nothing happens by mistake, and my serenity is directly influenced by my level of acceptance. I have to have the courage to address the things I can change in me.

"The wisdom to know the difference" is the issue most of us contend with. I suggest you seek out a spiritual mentor and explore this process on a personal level. Let's say that I'm driving down the highway and someone in another car speeds past me, so I speed up and pass him—and the game is on. The fact is, I can't control him or his car, but I do have control over my reaction and attitude. I can allow my negativity from childhood to live rent free in my mind and control my behavior, or I can recognize that I can't change the past, but I do have control of my recovery and my attitude. I can choose to just let that other driver pass me.

I say the Serenity Prayer several times daily because I must remind myself of what I do and don't have control over. Life is so much simpler and freedom is gained when I mind my own business.

We who lived in concentration camps can remember the men who walked through the huts comforting others, giving away their last piece of bread. They may have been few in number, but they offer sufficient proof that everything can be taken from a man but one thing: the last of the human freedoms—to choose one's attitude in any given set of circumstances, to choose one's own way.

Viktor Frankl

If I had remained frozen in my own little box, my own self-induced prison, I would never have broken out so that I could do something extraordinary in life. Today I believe in myself, and I believe in others. We live in the greatest country in the world, and we are blessed. So many choose to stay rooted to the ground only to wither and die. I suggest it is time for all of us to sprout wings and fly like eagles.

We all have the freedom to let go of the past and break out of our bondage of self and soar with the winners of life. Here is what we must do! **I**dentify our own self-bondage issues, **d**ecide to step over the line and do something positive, get **e**xcited, and then take **a**ction. It is a good IDEA!

You might be asking, "Can it be that simple?"
I say, "What if it is?"

Chapter 15

I Told Myself I Couldn't Do It—It Was a Lie!

Let others lead small lives, but not you.
Let others argue over small things, but not you.
Let others cry over small hurts, but not you.
Let others leave their future in someone else's hands, but not you.

Jim Rohn

What we tell ourselves in our self-talk counts—and it counts for a lot. We have all been programmed from the day we were born up until this moment. We have been programmed by parents, brothers and sisters, friends, teachers, clergy, radio, print media, and television. It is frightening how incredibly easy it is to get us to buy into these programming techniques. Most of this programming is the framework that forms our self-talk, and ultimately our self-worth.

When I was about six years old, I was drawing a picture of a house surrounded by trees with a swing set in the backyard. I was excited about my work and looked forward to showing it to my mom. However, when she saw the picture, she said, "You're a terrible artist. It is obvious that you can't draw." Conversely, she would tell me that I was a great athlete and that I would someday be in athletics for a living.

To this day, I have to struggle with self-talk when I draw. I have been involved in athletics my entire adult life—go figure! The fact of the matter is that she programmed me at a young age, and what she said is still in my consciousness decades later.

Television, radio, and print media program us minute after minute, day in and day out. We are persuaded to shop, feel, and even believe what they want us to believe. We are programmed for immediate gratification in our lives. Take a pill and feel better, pop the cap on a beer and beautiful women will appear, wear this and you will be a supermodel, super size, down size—it goes on and on.

What is it I am telling myself? What am I teaching my children? Does my self-talk motivate or deflate me? Does my self-talk allow me to dream big and know that I deserve to? Or am I telling myself I'm not worth it, I'm not good enough, smart enough, or talented enough? Is my self-talk keeping me in the rut, or am I using a positive version to build a ladder to climb out?

I had to stop myself from thinking negatively. The way I did this was to be willing to change. I identified the negativity and replaced the negatives with positives. I stopped these thoughts by telling myself, "That kind of thinking is not acceptable," and I immediately replaced the thought with a positive one. This was difficult at first but with persistence, over time it became very natural and even fun.

When I go to draw something, I tell myself that my mom's opinion and negative programming is not acceptable, and that I *can* draw. I tell myself that I am worthy of success, that my motivation to maximize my potential is of great importance, and that I do have something to offer others. I have changed my belief system, and it has allowed me freedom from self-bondage.

I used to have many voices in my head all talking at once. I have since eliminated all the personalities (voices) to four. I have identified the personalities that bid for attention in my thought process. First, there is the child—he is shy, playful, and silly. He dreams big dreams, and wants to explore and try anything and everything. Then there is the teenager—he is full of self-will, knows everything, and thinks about sex a lot. He is rebellious as well as embarrassed by the child personality.

Then I have the adult personality—he is in control. Practical and proper, he manages his emotions, wants to be successful, wants to be loved, and wants to look good. The adult tries to control the teenage personality but misses childhood freedom and fun.

Last is the judge. He is trying to weigh all sides of the arguments within my head. He is the logical one, the one in balance—and he has the last word.

It kind of goes like this: My child says when we go out today, "Let's wear our cowboy hat. It's cool." The teenager inside me says, "Are you crazy? People will laugh. We will look like an idiot." The adult says, "The hat really won't fit into the affair we will be attending. Even though I would love to wear my hat and it would be fun, maybe I won't fit in and I will be different." The judge evaluates the whole conversation and makes a decision.

Today I work through this process, and I have created a balance between the child, teenager, adult, and judge. I allow my child to play and my teenager to explore and be wild and adventurous. The adult gets to be mature and wise and giving, and the judge evaluates the results.

We all have some combination of these personalities in our lives; you may be able to think of others that influence you as well. I suggest you take a moment and identify your personalities and voices. Is any one personality dominant over the others, or are they equally balanced? Problems arise when the personalities are out of alignment—in which case you must begin to make program adjustments and changes. You will be surprised how easy this can be and how effective it is in our future success and serenity.

We will usually get exactly what we believe, so let's tell ourselves that we deserve to reach our dreams. This takes effort, action, and change, but this is truly the way of the warrior and the path to success. All of us have issues and life challenges—the difference is how we respond to the situation. Do we respond from the negative or the positive? Are we living in the problem rather than the solution?

Had I not raised my opinion of myself, I would have never gotten to the next level and above. I would still have been right where I was five, ten, fifteen years from now. This is not an overnight fix; it took and continues to take effort, focus, and willingness. I have to practice this self-talk in all of my affairs. I constantly have to stop for a moment and ask myself if I am reacting from a previously programmed message or from the new positive program. I suggest as we go, we take a moment every once in a while to pause and to change the program if necessary. A true warrior always seizes the moment for improvement and self-enlightenment!

We get so caught up in the little things in our lives and in our minds that we freeze up, run, or make excuses. It was time for me to stop majoring in the minors. I got off the bus and got into life. I continue to dream big and improve my belief system moment by moment!

For example, late afternoon on one bright and sunny day, I went to my key salesman and told him that we needed to make an additional $1,000 by the end of the evening. We were closing in four hours, and he told me it couldn't be done. I pointed my finger to his temple and said, "What if I tell you that I will blow your brains out if we do not make $1,000 by the close of the day?"

He replied, "In that case, consider it done"—and it was!

What changed in this scenario? It was all about motivation. It wasn't that he couldn't accomplish the task or that it was impossible; it was simply a matter of motivation. This is true for all of us. We say we can't or it's impossible usually because we aren't motivated. Had the motive been great enough, the task would have gotten done.

Imagine that I ask you to come up with $10,000 in two weeks. Most of us would say, "I can't do that." What if I offered some motivation such as your daughter needs surgery or she will die? I contend that you will get the money. What changed? Your motivation. The fact is, it can be done with powerful enough motivation.

Several years ago, I noticed my waist size had increased and my shirt size had gone from medium to large. I felt less energetic, and my lovely wife commented gently that I was gaining weight. I didn't pay much attention to this until they took an action picture of me for the school website. I looked at the picture and didn't recognize myself.

My stomach stuck out, I had two chins, and my face was puffy. I was shocked, and at that moment I decided I would lose the excess thirty-five pounds and keep it off, one day at a time. I was motivated.

I asked Bonnie to put me on a healthy diet, I increased my workout intensity, and I changed my self-talk. This wasn't easy, but within four months I was at my target weight. I looked and felt better, and I have kept the weight off ever since. I keep the picture of that fat guy and every now and again take a look at it as a reminder of what happens when I tell myself I am not worth it.

I have done many wrong things in my life, some of which I have shared with you in this book. I may have been wrong, but I did not remain that way. I realized that I could change and I could learn the way of the warrior so as to succeed at anything I desire.

I suggest we stop telling ourselves "we can't do it." I never tell myself I can't do it, as that's not the truth—that's a lie! Let's change our self-talk, and replace our old tapes with new and improved ones. Let's take steps *now* to be motivated, persistent, and successful. Those thousands of negative influences from TV, radio, print media, and so on must be replaced by positive programming. Read positive and uplifting motivational and educational books, listen to CDs, attend seminars and workshops, and find a mentor for guidance. This is the way of the warrior!

There are risks and costs to a program of action,
but they are far less than the long-range risks and costs of comfortable inaction.
John Fitzgerald Kennedy

Chapter 16

My Greatest Investment

When Bonnie and I decided to marry at the ripe old ages of eighteen and nineteen, we had a dream and we put together a plan for a successful and lifelong relationship. We realized that we needed to work together as a team, and that it wasn't going to be easy. We had to make some very difficult yet necessary decisions. We had to invest in our relationship and in our future.

Our investment wasn't monetary—we had no money. Our investment was directed towards our survival and future success. We decided that Bonnie needed to drop out of college and get a job to supplement my income, and I needed to go back to college to prepare for my career in law enforcement. This was an investment in ourselves as we understood our long-range goals for success depended on the steps we took at that moment. We couldn't afford electricity so we lived by candlelight with lots of blankets and cuddling. We invested our energy toward our dreams realizing that sacrifices had to be made.

Before we married, we'd decided on a few other matters of importance, and we planned accordingly. First we agreed that we would not have children for ten years so that we would first own our home and have insurance, successful careers, and money in the bank for emergencies. I put in my order for a girl first and a boy second, and we both agreed on a maximum of two children.

The next ten years Bonnie and I invested in our future family. We both worked and sacrificed to save money. We bought a house, acquired two cars, obtained insurance, and put money in the bank. Just over ten years after we married, Sheri was born, followed by Jason two years later. The investment we'd made in time and in our patience solidified the success of our family's future. We never gave up. Even when things were at their worst, we never, ever quit. We had a dream, we made a decision, we were excited, and we took action.

Bonnie and I have never taken a shortcut to success. We have worked hard and smart for everything we have. When I became a police officer, I was willing to invest my life for the sake of the safety and protection of others, and Bonnie was investing everything she could into our marriage knowing that I might not make it home some evening. Yet our dream was worth it.

When we decided to follow through with the martial arts studio, we had to make investments in ourselves as well. This included education, investigation, planning, and sacrifice of time and energy. I spent the time and money to educate myself and to prepare a plan of action. I utilized my mentors every step of the way. We traveled from one studio to another, taking notes on what was and wasn't working for them.

There was no limit to my dream or my purpose—nothing was going to crush the dream. I went to several influential friends and associates and raised enough capital in two weeks to open and fully equip my first karate studio. This location was only 1,100 square feet, but Bonnie and I made the inside the most professional, bright, and comfortable *dojo* in the area. It was small but mighty, and our investment paid off.

Within eight months, we grew out of that location and doubled the size of our facility. Once again we invested our money, time, and effort to make this location even better than the last. Five years later we did it again and doubled our facility—and five years after that we tripled our location size. Our current studio is 15,000 square feet and grosses well over one million dollars per year. Better yet, we teach and help thousands of people of every age, in and outside of our studio, to become the best they can be and to maximize their potential.

If we are going to reach our maximum potential, it is critical that we are willing to invest in our greatest asset—*ourselves*! There can be no shortcuts as the fundamentals are the foundation for future success. The day that each of my studios opened, they were completely ready for business—everything was in place and secured. When you walk into my studio, you realize right away that we care and that we are committed to our cause. There is no quitting, and there is no clause that allows us to run away!

However, in 2003, my business took a downward plunge and I went directly into panic mode. I met with Joe, a friend and a mentor, and told him my story of woe. I described a martial arts business seminar in Florida (three thousand miles away) that might be useful, but it would cost me $5,000 to make the trip. He reminded me that I always preach the necessity of investing in oneself and that it was time to put my money and my faith to work again. Joe was right, and I made the decision that my son and I would go to Florida for the seminar. That weekend I sought out mentorship and advice and got exactly what I needed. My investment paid off with dividends, and our business rocketed to the next level and beyond.

I have had to make the investment in good times and in bad. I owe this to myself, my family, and my God. I can tell you from my own experiences that if we want to succeed beyond our wildest dreams, we need to follow the path of those successful people who came before us and make the investment today because it will ultimately secure our freedom. We refused to use our children as an excuse for not doing something—rather they were the reason we did it. Sacrifices and investments were made to assure our family's future and our freedom.

Investing in ourselves takes effort, sacrifice, determination, and resolve. Nothing worth having is easy to achieve. I had to realize that the buck stopped with me, and I could either continue to find excuses or become a warrior!

Remember in the earlier chapters I said that motivation is one of the keys to my success? Unless I am willing to sacrifice and invest in myself, motivation will be smashed to death as will my hopes and dreams. I had to step outside of my self-inflicted bondage and go for the gusto. This is the only lifetime I will have. We are on this planet for such a short period of time, and it is our responsibility to do something extraordinary.

Half measures avail us nothing. This is so true. If I am only willing to put 50 percent into my hopes and dreams, I might as well keep digging my rut (grave) because that is the mindset of the masses and it is a recipe for failure. I was determined to be one of the few who actually do what it takes to give 100 percent. I invest the energy, time, money, blood, sweat, and tears to reach the next level of the warrior. I am not gifted, privileged, highly educated, or lucky—I am merely willing to make the necessary investment.

The only difference between the masses and the few is that the few are willing to step away from the average and follow the principles set forth by successful people. The few are willing to be human and step outside their comfort zone. The masses want to be comfortable even when they are miserable. The masses want to be secure, but not pay the price for freedom. The masses simply are lazy people with broken dreams. The few keep moving forward in good times and in bad. When they fall (and they do), they get back up and keep moving with a purpose and a resolve. The many quit, but the few never surrender!

All is not lost for the masses as all it takes is willingness—a willingness to take the actions necessary for change. We have to get sick and tired of being sick and tired and turn left through the open doors of greatness. The many can become one of the few if only they would identify their purpose, decide, get excited and enthusiastic, and take the necessary action.

Today, I am more teachable than ever because the benefits are so great. My AA sponsor tells me that being teachable is being spiritual. I suppose he means that when I am ready, God will appear; and when I am seeking answers, they will appear. I have uncovered and discovered that my serenity is directly proportional to my spiritual connection to my God. When I am full of self-righteous and self-centered motives, somehow, some way I am slammed right back down to being humble (or like I say, "right size"). I don't make excuses why I can't do it—I find reasons to make it happen.

In our martial arts studio, we hear every kind of excuse imaginable for why people can't sign up or why they are quitting. Most of these are smoke screens and have nothing to do with reality. I am amazed as to how many individuals and families say they can't afford the modest price of karate lessons. The benefits of the martial arts are worth the investment. Lives are saved, self-esteem and confidence increase, and people feel better overall. Yet so many people are simply not willing to make the investment for the future. I believe they are looking for immediate gratification but at all costs avoid the sacrifices it will take.

In our networking business, I hear the same smoke screen excuses over and over again. We met with a couple last night who wanted what we have; in fact, they are desperately looking for a "Plan B." When I told them that the investment was $300 to become a business owner and $100 per month for educational and business systems, and that they would have to read, listen to CDs, go to meetings, and step outside of their comfort zone, they immediately started putting up the smoke screens.

They said, "We can't afford it. We don't have the time. What if it doesn't work? Let us think about it." I related to what they were saying because I used to be the same way. I was in fear. I was afraid of the discomfort that change brings. I told myself I wasn't good enough or smart enough. I had no dream. I'd given up. How could I give up my television shows or my sporting events? (And what about my afternoon nap?)

I finally realized that all of those excuses are lies. I had to turn the television off, drink one less latté per day, stop spending money on my vices, and start budgeting to win. Time and money are the excuses the masses use to avoid reality. Yet I complained and whined about my lot in life. It is a shame, and it is shameful. The opportunities are so abundant for those who are willing to invest and go the extra mile.

I decided that it is better to be uncomfortable with being comfortable—that when I am comfortable for an extended period of time, I'm not growing any longer. Until I accepted that success in life demands and requires investment, I remained just one of the masses doomed to mediocrity. Yet today I am a warrior!

There are some basic principles for success that require investment. These require changes in our routines and in our thinking, but I assure you the investment we make today will more than pay for itself in the future. If you follow these simple principles, you will see daily positive results immediately.

1. **Purpose**—Dreams must stem from your purpose or the target has no value.

"Great minds have purpose, others have wishes."
Washington Irving

2. **Effort**   *There is no substitute for hard work.*
Thomas Edison

I'm a great believer in luck, and the harder I work, the more I have of it.
Thomas Jefferson

*Opportunity is missed by most people
because it comes dressed in overalls and looks like work.*
Thomas Edison

3. **Be Teachable**   *When the student is ready, the teacher will appear.
When the teacher is ready, the student will appear.*

4. **Mentorship**
*To live a balanced life, each person should have both a mentor and a mentee.
We must be engaged in learning and teaching if we are to remain vital.*
George E. Toles, President, The Toles Company

5. **Reading Program**—Read a minimum of fifteen minutes per day. Read inspirational and educational materials.

6. **CD Program**—Listen to educational audio materials at least once per day. Utilize your commute to and from your job for education.

7. **Seminars/Clinics/Workshops**—Attend educational seminars for continued support, direction, and ideas.

8. **Affirmations**—Use positive affirmations and self-talk throughout your day. Create good vibrations in your head, not negative ones.

9. **Be Accountable**—Be accountable to your mission in life, to your plan for success, to your family, and to your mentors. Most of all, be accountable to *you*.

This above all: To thine own self be true.
William Shakespeare

10. **Be Grateful**—Seize and embrace the moments in your life. Find the blessings rather than the problems. Live in the solutions, not the insanity. At the end of each day, take an inventory of the areas in your life that need improvement, list your many blessings, and be grateful.

Here are a few other practices to keep you focused on a daily basis:

1. **Morning Meditation**—Take a moment each morning for meditation and visualization. Take in a few deep breaths and listen. When you breathe in, take the breath into your stomach and not your chest. Your stomach should expand when you breathe in and deflate upon exhale. Visualize a positive and productive day full of friendship, success, and love.

2. **Morning Reading**—Each morning before you get going, take a few minutes and read something of inspiration—some kind of quote or thought for the day.

3. **At Bedtime**—Take a moral inventory of your day. Assess your successes and failures, and ask yourself if you have done or said anything that requires amends. If so, make sure the next day that you take care of resolving it.

4. Be Responsible

Hold yourself responsible for a higher standard than anybody expects of you. Never excuse yourself.

Henry Ward Beecher

These principles are the road map to happiness and success. Rarely has a person failed who has thoroughly followed these success and life principles. It will take an effort on your part and a willingness to change. I suggest you practice these things each and every day for the next twelve months. If your life has not improved drastically, then go back to the way you were.

Once again, let's stop investing our energy and our resources on changing others and spend that energy on ourselves. We should decide what needs to be changed within us and change it. As we begin to change and grow, we will be amazed at how the world around us gets better and better each and every moment. Our attitude and our positive behavior will attract people rather than repel them. By living life with principles, we create a force for success and greatness.

The fact is, that to do anything in the world worth doing, we must not stand back shivering and thinking of the cold and danger, but jump in and scramble through as well as we can.

Robert Cushing

Chapter 17

Experience, Strength, Hope

I have shared much with you openly and candidly about my life experiences, the strength that I have developed, and the message of hope. I have been to hell and back; I have struggled with addictions and failure, but I never gave up. I never surrendered, and as a result my dreams are coming true.

I refuse to rest on my laurels, and I continue to be of service to others. Today I am a nice guy and honest man with integrity and purpose. When I rest my head on my pillow at night, I fall asleep peacefully without guilt or regrets. When I do something wrong, I repair it as soon as possible, and I stay "right size."

Of course, being human, I do have moments when I fall back into old behaviors. Last year we took a wonderful cruise along the northeast coast of the United States and Canada. We ended our trip with a one-week stay in New York. The vacation was spectacular with the changing of the colors from summer to fall—it was amazing!

My in-laws joined Bonnie and me for the trip, and their company was a blessing. We get along so well with Bonnie's parents; they are fun to be with. My mother-in-law, Shirley, is full of energy and very funny. We kid each other a lot, and she is an inspiration to me. My father-in-law, Leo, and I have bonded as both friends and family.

In New York, we went sightseeing and visited relatives—it was nice. We had to extend our trip a few days because Shirley's sister passed away while we were there so we stayed for the funeral. This created some stress, but we were grateful that we could lend our support and love to the rest of the family.

The last day of our trip, while I was at the check-in counter for our rental car, I had one of those human moments. The girl behind the counter said something that didn't set right with me, and I reacted. My reaction was filled with anger and self-righteous indignation. I abused this woman verbally and embarrassed my family.

It didn't matter who was right and who was wrong. My behavior was not one of kindness and compassion. I had allowed my old tapes to kick in. This was a human moment, but inexcusable. I spoke with my mentor about the incident, and he suggested I write a letter to the company and make amends for my behavior, which I immediately did. He also reminded me that an apology must be followed by correct action, meaning this could not happen again.

I learn from my mistakes and inappropriate behavior, I gain strength from my ability to correct my errors, and I gain hope for the future. It requires humility and the ability to change. Sometimes it requires all my strength to do what is right, but in the long run I experience the blessings for correct actions.

I cleared away the past and today live life anew. I let go of all resentments, as they are death to my dreams. I let go and move on. The past is my experiences, today is my present, and tomorrow is my future. I am responsible for today, this very moment. When I live in the past, I will not gain strength, and I waste today.

Look not mournfully into the past, it comes not back again.
Wisely improve the present, it is thine. Go forth to meet the shadowy future
Without fear and with a strong heart.
Henry Wadsworth Longfellow

It is always my responsibility to admit when I am wrong; I make what I call a "living amends." If I yell at my wife, saying "sorry" over and over again without making a change in my behavior is not an amends. I must follow through with action by making a living amends and ensuring I do not repeat that behavior in the future. I identify my defects of character and continually make corrections; otherwise my apologies are without substance. Even though I am bound to make mistakes, it is within my power and control to move past the difficulties, make repairs where necessary, and move on. I stopped beating myself up for being human. A warrior knows we should aim for progress rather than perfection.

Fractures well cured make us more strong.

Ralph Waldo Emerson

As I begin to repair and rebuild, it is my responsibility to give it away. By my actions I will attract those who want what I have. By stepping outside of self and carrying the message to others, I continue the way of the warrior. By example and by teaching, I model strength and hope. I can't keep what I don't give away—this is a universal law! I ask myself, "What is it that I have to give to others? What is the example I am setting? Am I attracting positive people? Is my path one that others will wish to follow? Will my life be a blessing?"

The ultimate measure of a man is not where he stands in moments of comfort,
But where he stands at times of challenge and controversy.

Martin Luther King, Jr.

I can either allow my past to destroy me or make me stronger. I choose to fight back and to be free from worry and want. As a young child, I made the decision that the buck stopped with me—that I was going to achieve great and wonderful things in my life. I decided that I would change from mediocrity to success and freedom. I wouldn't be destroyed by my habits, addictions, fears, insecurities, and character defects. I am more determined today to never, ever surrender my dreams to anyone or anything!

Our experiences are the sum total of whom and what we are today. We have made good and bad choices along the way. Our experiences have given us strength and weaknesses. We must not ignore these lessons—we must learn from them. We have learned that by applying success principles and taking the proper steps to achieve greatness, we can overcome anything life has to throw at us.

As we begin to see more clearly our purpose and our dreams, we will be able to put our experiences to good use and gain insight and strength. As we move from the believing to the knowing, we will gain hope and faith. It will take a conscious effort and willingness for change, but we can do it. If I can, you can!

I have had the awesome privilege of seeing hundreds of people's lives make a complete 180-degree turn for the better. I have seen this with men and women who get sober and work the steps outlined in AA. I have seen them put their marriages back together, gain custody of their children, and become successful members of society. This is truly a blessing, but they had to work for it, and today they live it.

In my karate studio and in my network business, I have seen the same 180-degree change in thousands of people. It is amazing what people are capable of when they have a purpose and a plan of action.

Lya started her study of karate with me in 1999. She came in a broken-down woman with no self-esteem or confidence. She was being abused in her marriage and had lost all her strength and hope for the future. Her dreams and her passion were smashed. After a few months of lessons and some guidance from me, she started to take control of her life. She began to walk and talk with more confidence and self-esteem.

Lya cried in nearly every class, and if I looked into her eyes outside of class, she would break out in tears. Nonetheless she never quit; instead she persevered and followed the path less traveled. She divorced that guy and took custody of her three children. She lost fifty pounds and earned her Black Belt. She went on to work full-time at my studio for a number of years and gained the love and respect of students, parents, and colleagues alike. Better yet, she respects herself and has become the woman she always wanted to be. Lya sets an example of experience, strength, and hope. She is the model of the impact of the willingness to overcome and to change everything, and she continues to grow.

Another student of mine, Wendy, was also close to being a lost cause. Abused by her husband and completely deflated, she was mild and meek without the will to go on. She had two young children, little money, and no hope. Wendy decided one day to start classes. She said she was sick and tired of being sick and tired, and she needed help. She went through the 180-degree transformation. She divorced her husband and has raised two very happy kids. She works to support her family and is a Black Belt. If these two women can do it, so can you!

I will fight the dream stealers, and I will win. I will fight the masses and refuse to allow their negative programming to squash my freedom. I will battle the negative forces within me, and I will conquer them. I will not be influenced by the media or the forces that constantly are trying to destroy my dreams. I will associate with the winners and pray for the losers. I will continue to learn and then give it away!

I will continue to be the man I have always wanted to be and improve on that. I will gain strength from my experiences and keep the hope and the faith alive. You can't take this from me because it is my passion, my mission, and my purpose in life. Tell me I can't, and I will show you I will! Tell me it won't work, and I will make it work! Tell me it's impossible and I will show you the possible!

The chances are that you have already come to believe that happiness is unattainable. But men have attained it. And they have attained it by realizing that happiness does not spring from the procuring of physical or mental pleasure, But from the development of reason and the adjustment of conduct to principles.

from *How to Live on 24 Hours a Day* by Arnold Bennett

As I said earlier, we have to get good and mad and be willing to fight for our freedom just as the men and women have on the battlefields. Let's stand up and take notice of our opportunities and seize the path of the warrior. Let's stop living in the problem and find solutions. It's time to stop blaming and take responsibility. Stand with the few or fall with the many—it's your choice.

I am determined to make right choices. I can make a difference in my life and in the lives of those around me. I can do and be whomever I choose, negative or positive.

I constantly uncover and discover paths for reaching my next level of success; the doors are open if I am aware and willing. It's important I always look for the next level on my path as a warrior seeking out the next peak to challenge my resolve. I can never be satisfied—I always look to improve and grow. I want to be of service to others, and be a warrior. Whether in good times or bad, I see what I can do for others.

If you have much, give of your wealth; if you have little, give of your heart.

Arab Proverb

Chapter 18

Dream "Mission Possible"

Some of the world's greatest feats were accomplished by people not smart enough to know they were impossible.

Doug Larson

Martin Luther King, Jr. said, "I have a dream"—and the world listened. It is time to start dreaming once again, for without a dream the mission is impossible. Dreamers dream big and believe with all their heart that the mission is possible.

We *can* achieve our dreams! I have seen it happen hundreds of times. Determination, perseverance, and accountability are vital to achieving dreams. A "never quit" attitude and a willingness to do whatever it takes, even when life gets in the way, are required.

Liz came into my studio ten years ago with her father. At that time she was in her mid-twenties and both mentally and physically challenged. Her father signed her up for classes, and Liz fell in love with our program. Unfortunately, her father's perception of what Liz was capable of was flawed. He didn't think she could handle the physical and mental aspects that karate requires, so he stopped paying her tuition. At this time, Liz was totally dependent on her father for money and shelter.

Having a dream and a purpose, Liz came to me and asked what tuition would cost. I gave her the prices, and she left my office. One week later she came back in and notified me that she had found a job at a local grocery store. She handed me a check for one month of tuition. One month later, Liz came in and paid for her program in full. She told me she was determined to be a Black Belt, and she wasn't quitting.

Today, Liz is a second-degree Black Belt and has a good job at the same grocery store. She lives in her own apartment and teaches at our karate studio. Liz is a perfect example that the "mission is possible." She had every reason not to continue and to give up, yet she had a dream and was willing to do whatever it took to reach her goals and objectives.

Most people who succeed in the face of seemingly impossible conditions are people who simply don't know how to quit.

Robert Schuller

Ted came into my studio one week after I opened for business. He was in a wheelchair, permanently paralyzed from the chest down from an automobile accident. However, at the age of twenty-one, Ted wasn't ready to give up.

He asked me if I could teach him how to protect himself and to help him develop his mind, body, and spirit. I had no idea what I could do for him, yet I said, "Let's get started right away." I sought out information as to how I could best serve Ted, and after a few months we were seeing progress. Ted had his challenges, and without a doubt he could have used his injury as an excuse, yet he was determined not to quit.

Ted became a high-ranking brown belt and went on to a successful career. He also plays several other sports. There were many obstacles along the way; but as a team, the mission was possible.

One afternoon his wife came in to me very frustrated. Every evening, Ted would insist that she drag him up the stairs even though we all knew he could do it himself. I told her it was a matter of motivation and made a suggestion. I told her that she should go to the top of the stairs, take off all her clothes, then stand there and invite Ted to join her in the bedroom. This would create a sense of excitement and motivation.

She came in the next day and said that Ted took one look at her naked body at the top of the stairs and crawled up the stairs in a flash. She also said that the rest of the evening was wonderful. It wasn't that the mission to climb the stairs was impossible—it was simply a matter of laziness, and as long as his wife was catering to him, the motivation wasn't great enough. Ted never has given up, and his inspiration and his success have helped hundreds of paraplegics around the world.

When I was medically retired from the police department, I was depressed and confused. All my education and dreams were wrapped up in my career as a law enforcement officer, and I had no idea what to do next. My wife was working full-time while I was sitting around in my own misery and self-pity. Then one of my mentors pulled me aside one day and said, "Get a job."

I asked, "Doing what?"

He replied, "It doesn't matter—just do something. I don't care if you are sweeping floors or cleaning toilets, just get moving and stop using your wife."

I cried out, "I was a professional police officer. I can't take a job as a janitor or a hamburger flipper."

He replied, "Then stay in your rut and keep digging." He told me that I can choose to do anything I want if I was willing to accept the consequences.

I realized he was right, and I got a job the next day stocking paint at a local paint store. I understood that my self-worth had been challenged, and in order to right the ship, I had to swallow my ego and get into action. Action breeds action, and laziness breeds laziness.

I stopped sitting around in my own self-pity after it was suggested that I get off my butt and do *something*. I had to stop relying on others to co-sign my crap. It was time to be responsible and accountable.

I suppose I was waiting for something to happen—like my mom used to say, "Someday our ship will come in." I say that I need to swim out and tug that ship to shore because nothing is free. I have to work for it. I had to invest the time, the energy, the money, and the effort— otherwise I would have continued to get only what I had always gotten.

Ah come on, Adrian, it's true. I was nobody. But that don't matter either,
you know? 'Cause I was thinkin', it really don't matter if I lose this fight.
It really don't matter if this guy opens my head, either,
'cause all I wanna do is go the distance.
Nobody's ever gone the distance with Creed, and if I can go that distance,
you see, and that bell rings and I'm still standin',
I'm gonna know for the first time in my life, see, that
I weren't just another bum from the neighborhood."
from the movie *Rocky*

Rocky was just another one of the many until he decided to go the distance. He had to train day in and day out. He trained physically, mentally, and spiritually. Nobody gave him a chance to win. They continued to try to steal his dream away. Rocky had a dream and a purpose, and he answered the call by taking action. He never gave up. Even when beaten down and broken, he got back up and fought the "Impossible Mission" until he convinced everyone that dreams do come true—even for the bum from the streets. And although the Rocky character is fiction, the true life story of how Sylvester Stallone starred in and made this movie parallels it very accurately. Stallone never gave up, and his persistence and determination coupled with hard work made his dream come true.

You're 5 foot nothin', 100 and nothin', and you have barely a speck of
athletic ability.
And you hung in there with the best college football players in the land for
two years.

And you're gonna walk outta here with a degree from the University of Notre Dame.

In this life, you don't have to prove nothin' to nobody but yourself.

from the movie *Rudy*

After that "talking to," Rudy Ruettiger went back out onto the football field for Notre Dame and played the last thirty seconds of his last home game of the season. He tackled the opposing quarterback, causing Notre Dame to win the game. At the end of the game, Rudy was carried off the field on the shoulders of his teammates. He had to prove to himself that he could achieve his dream even though everyone around him, including his family, told him that his mission was impossible.

My family and I had the pleasure of meeting Rudy a few years ago, and we were extremely impressed with his passion and determination. While I was talking with Rudy, he had a "human moment." Let me explain—I told Rudy that we were Black Belts and owned one of the most successful studios in North America.

Rudy said to us, "I always wanted to train in the martial arts, but I am a little old and out of shape right now, and I don't think I could do it."

I laughed and said, "Rudy, you played football for Notre Dame. You are the one that says dreams can come true and nothing is impossible."

He laughed and said, "You're right! I can do it!"

"There is no use trying," said Alice; "One can't believe impossible things."
"I dare say you haven't had much practice," said the Queen.
"When I was your age, I always did it for half an hour a day.
Why, sometimes I've believed as many as six impossible things before breakfast."

Lewis Carroll—from *Alice's Adventures in Wonderland*

Chapter 19
Unleashing Our "Inner Warrior"

If something comes to life in others because of you,
then you have made an approach to immortality.

Norman Cousins

A warrior is one who serves. I became a police officer to protect and serve. I knew from a very early age that I felt best when I was helping others. I remember in high school that I was always protecting and standing up for the students being bullied and taken advantage of. It has been my lifetime purpose to protect, teach, and serve.

Being a warrior can take many forms, but the bottom line is living for something greater than self. You can't be arrogant and selfish and still be successful. When we concentrate on what we can do for our fellows, rather than what we can do for ourselves, the more successful we will be.

Many years ago I opened a second martial arts studio. We redesigned the physical appearance of the studio as well as the services we would offer to our students and families. We met with all the students and parents and outlined our commitment to them and their training. Within a few months, the studio was prospering and everyone was pleased with the services we offered. We delivered what we had promised, and we were being warriors!

Because of the distance between my two schools, I decided to sell the new facility to a fellow Black Belt from my original studio. Immediately, this individual decided that he knew what he was doing and no longer would take direction from me. Even though we had developed a proven system for success, he remained determined to reinvent the wheel. His students and parents began calling me and complaining that they were being mistreated and their wishes were being ignored.

Within a few months, the studio was going downhill rapidly, but he still wouldn't take direction. I received a telephone call one Saturday advising me that students showed up for classes and found the facility empty with nothing more than a phone book in the middle of the floor. Of course this was a shock and a disappointment. Students and parents were angry and upset with good reason. I spoke with my attorney and was advised that I was not liable, but the tuition money the students had paid was lost. I couldn't justify this outcome because I am a warrior—my purpose is to help, not harm others.

I took inventory of the money owed to the students and their families along with any outstanding bills and set out to repay the entire debt. I ended up paying well over $100,000 in refunds and expenses out of my own pocket. I did this because success is directly proportional to my willingness, my integrity, and my accountability. Even though I had no ownership in the studio, I felt responsible to my industry and to the students and parents who had placed their trust and their money with one of my former students.

The fragrance always remains on the hand that gives the rose.

Gandhi

I don't say this to impress you, but rather to impress upon you the importance of being a warrior in *all* affairs. Success and happiness achieved will ultimately be determined by our actions, not our intentions. Help and assist others to greatness, and you too will achieve greatness. It is by giving we receive; yet so many of us miss this step because we are driven by self-will run riot.

I have taught thousands of martial artists over the years. Hundreds have achieved the rank of black belt, yet only a few of these black belts have ever become true warriors. Despite all their physical talents, many of these students couldn't grasp the very essence of "the one who serves." Their focus was turned inward, demanding that they be taught, that they achieve, that they win, and that they wear the black belt.

The many Black Belts who are still teaching and passing on the blessing of being a warrior are true and mighty warriors. The ones who remain with me understand that the black belt has no meaning or worth if the lessons learned are not passed on. We remember our roots and our struggles, and we reach out to assist others during their journey.

These Black Belts are men and women who give of themselves unconditionally, and I can assure you that each of them is healthy and happy in mind, body, and spirit. They have found success in their professions and in their personal lives all because they know that success is gained by giving and not taking. Those who never came to understand are wandering place to place, looking for what the world owes them—and wondering why they are not healthy in mind, body, and spirit.

Only a life lived for others is a life worthwhile.

Albert Einstein

A warrior is relentless and never deterred from his/her primary purpose. A warrior sees obstacles as challenges and sees situations rather than problems. A warrior understands that there will be rough times and simple times, and each one needs to be handled with the warrior's full effort. A warrior lives his life, and sometimes dies, to be of service to others. Warriors do this with honesty, integrity, and purpose—and with no regret.

A warrior never rests on her laurels. She is always on guard and ready to battle the odds for "right." She has a plan of action and a strong desire to succeed. She sees the enemy and challenges the enemy's spirit. The warrior has many sleepless nights and lives with pain of the body, mind, and spirit, yet he never gives up. A warrior builds his team with other like-minded warriors who are willing to pay the price for success.

Warriors refuse the easy and relish the challenge. Never overcome by the task or by laziness, they have no time for hesitation. The warrior learns and studies with great and wise warriors who have fought the battles before her, and she is fortified with their strength and their experience. The warrior accumulates knowledge and experience and along the way teaches it to others so they too will become the ones who serve.

When I think of a warrior, I am reminded of a former student of mine, Brandon Hampson. Even though his life was tragically cut short, he left a lasting legacy which I believe is the definition of a true warrior. Here are my thoughts published in our June 2005 newsletter.

" 'I would like to introduce you to American Martial Arts Academy's newest and honored Shodan—1st degree Black Belt—20-year-old Mr. Brandon Hampson.'

"These are the words I spoke during a very special Black Belt ceremony on June 22, 2005, in the Hampsons' home. As I and Mrs. Wenneberg and other senior Black Belts gathered around Brandon while he rested on his bed, I couldn't help but reflect on Leadership. You see, Brandon began his journey with AMAA in 1999, and over the time that we have had the honor of sharing his life, he has shown himself to be a true warrior.

"Brandon has always been enthusiastic, full of energy, joy, humor, and an uplifting attitude. He has always been respectful, courteous, generous of spirit, and helping in nature. Although he has had the personal challenge of being hearing-impaired, he never allowed this to negatively influence his efforts or attitude. In class, he always gave 110 percent. He stayed focused and persistent and advanced steadily through the ranks. He assisted the instructors, participated in our specific classes (like weapons), and attended studio activities (like Idyllwild). He always had a 'Black Belt' attitude, and his grace and smile have persisted even through the most horrific of times during the last nine months.

"In September of 2004, Brandon was diagnosed with a brain tumor which has subsequently proved to be a particularly aggressive form of cancer. Since that day, though, Brandon has shown his usual good attitude, humor, and courage in the face of four major brain surgeries, numerous painful procedures and treatments, radiation, chemotherapy, paralysis and seizures. He has amazed all his health care professionals with his zest for life and his good nature and determination."

"As I stood next to Brandon, it was obvious that he had fought a good fight against this horrible disease; and although he is now terminal, the light shines bright in Brandon's eyes and the courage of his spirit can be felt. As I bowed and respectfully handed Brandon his new Black Belt and conferred upon him the rank of Shodan in Goju Shin-Ryu, I knew that the lessons I, and others, had received from Brandon would stay with us forever. Looking into his eyes, pupil to pupil, we both knew that leadership goes both ways and we have learned from each other.

"Leadership is not a gift; you must earn it with your very actions. We lead by how we behave, by our attitude, by our contributions to the world as a whole. We have the opportunity for negative or positive leadership on each and every day. It is in our own hands. Brandon has led through his consistent and unyielding integrity with positive, ethical character, good humor, persistent effort, and undefeatable courage. He has demonstrated what a Black Belt is by being the best he can be even through the most dreadful of times.

"We are ultimately judged by the way we have lived our life. Brandon's life is a blessing and a way of courage and leadership. His leadership lives today and forever. I encourage you to learn from his example and to take on the responsibility of leadership no matter the challenges encountered."

Mr. Hampson passed away on June 26, 2005, at 20 years of age.

Let's be people of service—to our parents, our spouse and children, brothers and sisters, friends and co-workers, even strangers. We should lend a helping hand instead of expecting a handout. As I have said before, living life successfully is not for the weak of heart—it is for the strong. When we go to school or work tomorrow, instead of looking for what others can do for us, let's ask what we can do for them. We should do this expecting nothing in return, and do it every day for the rest of our lives. Going the extra mile today will assure us of success tomorrow.

A warrior does not have to be physically strong or even possess any special talents. She merely has to be a person who is willing to live for something greater than herself. The battle is between our ears and the eighteen-inch journey from our brains to our hearts. Unless we realize that we can't just *think* our way into being a warrior and must instead *act* our way into it, we will never have the connection between head and heart.

All success consists in this: You are doing something for somebody—
benefiting humanity—and the feeling of success comes from the
consciousness of this.

Elbert Hubbard

I asked one of my mentors once how I would know if I was successful. Would riches come to me? Would I receive all the things that I wanted? Would I live to a ripe old age? How would I know?

As usual, he had the answer: "You will realize success from moment to moment. It will be that feeling inside that creates harmony and peace. Instead of the knot in the stomach or in the neck, you will feel restful. Your mind will be free from anger and resentments and will overflow with gratitude. You will intuitively handle things that used to baffle you. At night you will rest your head on your pillow and find serenity, peace, and hope."

He went on to say that I might find great wealth and many of my wants might come true; but these things are not, and shall never be, the measure of a person's success. Rather, the way the person has lived his or her life will be the true measure. You can be evil, with or without wealth, and you can do great deeds, broke or rich.

What I do with God's blessings and gifts will ultimately be my failure or my success. Money is not evil; it is the love of money that is evil. It is not having great material wealth that is evil; it is the flaunting of such blessings that is evil.

As he spoke those words, I began to understand more clearly my purpose and the importance of being a warrior. I realized that everything I own, everything I possess—body, mind, and spirit—can be taken away from me at any time, but the good I have done, the battles I have fought, and the difference I have made will last forever.

Living a life of abundance is not a bad thing, but living a life of arrogance is a crime. We deserve to live life at its fullest; we deserve riches, love and friendships, but only if we are willing to pay the price. Looking for our blessings to be hand-delivered is the mindset of the masses, and I refuse to fall into that trap because I am a warrior.

I will fight for my right to be free, and I will fight for your right to be free. I will fortify my stance with the knowledge and experience of my mentors, and I will meet challenges with resolve and with purpose.

We must pledge our allegiance to our purpose and our mission in life and refuse to allow the dream stealers to win the battle of mediocrity. We must stand tall with our shoulders upright and our eyes focused. We must listen and learn and take the road less traveled. It is the warrior within us who will ultimately surrender to die or fight to win.

The sole meaning of life is to serve humanity.

Leo Tolstoy

The message of the warrior, "one who serves," is without question our number-one priority here on earth. I know that my happiness and my success in life are a direct result of my being a warrior. It certainly isn't because of my great looks, my intelligence, my childhood, or my luck. I am nothing special, and as I have shared with you, I have had great challenges along the way, but I never quit because I had dreams and a purpose.

Because of my willingness to go through the open doors of opportunity and learn from the wisdom of others, I now know the path to success—the one I have clearly outlined for you in previous chapters. That is the Yellow Brick Road to massive success in all areas of your life.

However, if you recall in *The Wizard of Oz*, Dorothy had to help others during her journey. She stopped to help the Scarecrow to find a heart, the Tin Man to find a brain, and the Cowardly Lion to find courage. Sure, her primary purpose was to get back to Kansas, but when you look at the story, you realize that had she not stopped long enough to help others, she would have never achieved her goal of going home.

Dorothy faced many obstacles that were intended to misdirect her from her primary purpose, but with determination and focus, plus a plan and mindset of a warrior, she remained on course. She and her friends learned that through their efforts as a team, with a primary purpose and determination, all of their dreams came true. The space between their ears finally reached their hearts, and they found happiness, success, and peace.

Great opportunities to help others seldom come,
but small ones surround us daily.

Sally Koch

Our souls are hungry for meaning, for the sense that we have figured out
How to live so that our lives matter, so that the world will be at least a
Little bit different for our having passed through it.

Rabbi Harold S. Kushner

Chapter 20

Attitude of Gratitude

The hardest arithmetic to master is that which enables us to count our blessings.

Eric Hoffer

In my twelve-step program, steps four and five deal with making an inventory of ourselves and sharing this inventory with God and another trusted person. In this inventory, everything about me was revealed. I listed my good and bad qualities, not leaving anything out. I shared my deepest, darkest secrets, and I listed people I had harmed as well as those I had resentments against.

This inventory and sharing with my mentor and with my God revealed my true nature and allowed me to focus on truth rather than my distorted view of myself. My mentor listened carefully to my life's story and guided me to a new and improved attitude. He suggested that rather than dwelling on the negatives of my childhood, I should look for the good and positive experiences. I meditated on this concept and began to immediately remember some of the positives of my childhood. I remembered how loving my mother was, and how she used to dance around the house to the music of the 1950s. She would sing and whistle and encourage us to join in.

My mother was always there for me and truly tried to create harmony. I remember after my mom got ill with a terminal disease, how she and I would stay up late into the night. We talked and watched Johnny Carson on television. We laughed and shared and cried together—it was a wonderful time. I remembered the way she encouraged me to seek out my dreams, telling me I could be successful if I wanted it badly enough.

Even during the most difficult of times, my mother was my biggest believer and inspiration. She knew that I would be successful and that one day I would discover my inner warrior.

With this simple change in my attitude, I began to feel gratitude rather than anger and resentment. I applied the simple technique of replacing negatives with positives in all areas of my life, and I experienced a complete transformation from a negative person to one with an attitude of gratitude.

Let us be grateful to people who make us happy;
they are the charming gardeners who make our souls blossom.

Marcel Proust

I attend my twelve-step meetings in order to maintain my sobriety and to help others still suffering. I also attend so that I can remember where I have come from and because I must remain grateful. I could have lost everything of value to me because of my self-centered, ungrateful behavior, and this is why I must always have gratitude.

I must focus on the positives in my life—having good relationships, a roof over our heads, food in our bellies, and an abundance of opportunities. The more directly I am focused toward the positive, the more positive things will be attracted to me.

There was a time in my life when I took my wife, my children, my friends, and even my sobriety for granted. I forgot to see the good in things and focused on my resentments and anger. I looked around and saw what I wanted. I noticed that others were getting all the breaks, which made me feel I was being persecuted. I had the "poor me" syndrome that affects the masses of today. Poor me, poor me—pour me another drink!

With this attitude of poor me, I did drink again and began to spin out of control once more. I nearly destroyed my marriage, my career, and my friendships. Had I not swallowed my ego, changed my negative actions to positive ones, stopped the destructive behavior, and gotten back to being a warrior, I was doomed for failure and death.

I made a call to my mentor while in a drunken stupor and asked for help. He asked me if I was ready to follow directions and to go to any lengths to change my life. I said yes. By the time he got me to the emergency room, I went into heart failure and life-saving measures had to be taken. As I lay there wondering if I was going to die, I made a decision to take any and all action needed to be successful—no matter what.

They say that we all have a moment of clarity sometime in our life—some call it a spiritual awakening. While I was recovering in the hospital, I had one of those powerful moments. I was sitting alone in the break room late one evening feeling sorry for myself. One of the nurses came in and asked if I wanted to pray with her. Not a big believer in prayer, I hesitated, and then remembered that I had promised I would go to any lengths.

She held out both her hands palm up and I rested my hands in hers. She began to pray in Spanish, and even though I didn't understand what she was saying, I felt the warmth of comfort and peace come over my body. I began to cry uncontrollably and rested my head on the table. I then felt her massaging my shoulders as I cried. After five minutes or so, I lifted my head, and as I turned around to thank her, I was stunned to see that Caleb, my friend from work, was the one rubbing my shoulders rather than the nurse.

I asked Caleb where the nurse had gone, and he replied, "What nurse? I've been here for several minutes and no one has been in here." He added that he hadn't seen anyone leaving the room as he walked in. You might be saying that I was probably hallucinating. Whatever the case, I can assure you that it was a moment that changed me from the inside out. I felt a power of something greater than myself—a power that made me feel whole and not alone anymore.

Whether you believe or not is not the point. I suggest that we be ready and open to our minds and hearts for spiritual awakenings. It is powerful, and it is a gift for which I will be forever grateful.

Gratitude is our most direct line to God and the angels.
If we take the time, no matter how crazy and troubled we feel,
We can find something to be thankful for.
The more we seek gratitude, the more reason the angels
Will give us for gratitude and joy to exist in our lives.

Terry Lynn Taylor

Happiness, success, and dreams are achieved in direct proportion to our ability to be grateful. Being miserable and ungrateful is ugly and destructive, and it attracts the negative. Gratitude will bring us peace and serenity in this complicated life.

At this very moment, I am looking out into my *dojo* area, and I am so grateful to see the children working with my son and his instructors. The parents are sitting in our Serenity area, which has a peaceful waterfall and plants for their comfort. The parents and their children are smiling and enjoying the moment. My daughter is with the students in our after-school program helping them to become the best they can be. As I focus on their happiness, I have a sense of overwhelming gratitude.

When people walk into our academy for the first time, I want them to be overcome with a sense of caring and appreciation. I want them to feel the warmth, genuine respect, and honor in which we approach them. I am told time after time by our students that even though they may have had a bad day, they immediately feel better when they walk in because of our attitude of gratitude and caring.

We must live our life as a blessing, reaching out to others as a warrior and being grateful for the opportunities that have been made available to us. When we walk and talk and demonstrate in all our affairs a sense of gratitude, we are changing the lives of others even if it's just for a moment.

What if you gave someone a gift and they neglected to thank you for it—
Would you be likely to give them another? Life is the same way.
In order to attract more of the blessings that life has to offer,
You must truly appreciate what you already have.

Ralph Marston

I often get an orange juice from the same store in the morning. The checkout person Mike is young and bored with life. The first time we met, he asked how I was, and I replied, "I have never been better."

He was shocked but said, "That's cool." I asked how he was and he said "Okay—bored and tired."

After a few days of this same exchange of words, his attitude began to shift. It was on a Monday morning when I asked Mike, "How are you today, my friend?"

He replied, "It's a great day."

I looked at him and said, "Thank you, Mike. You have put a smile on my face and your attitude has recharged my spiritual batteries. I appreciate it."

He smiled and asked, "Really?" I assert that we *can* change ourselves and the world with a smile. To this very day, Mike greets me and others with a smile and a positive affirmation.

The deepest craving of human nature is the need to be appreciated.

William James

Let us rise up and be thankful, for if we didn't learn a lot today, at least we learned a little,
And if we didn't learn a little, at least we didn't get sick,
And if we got sick, at least we didn't die; so, let us all be thankful.

Buddha

Here is what I did—I focused on an attitude of gratitude every day for thirty days. By the end of the first day I felt more relaxed and slept sounder. By the end of the thirty days, it was clear that I was a happier and more serene person, and many of my aches and pains of body and mind had disappeared. I am sincerely grateful, and I became a stronger warrior as a result.

Gratitude unlocks the fullness of life.
It turns what we have into enough, and more.
It turns denial into acceptance, chaos to order, confusion to clarity.
It can turn a meal into a feast, a house into a home, a stranger into a friend.
Gratitude makes sense of our past, brings peace for today,
and creates a vision for tomorrow.

Melody Beattie

Chapter 21

Budo—"The Way"

Given enough time, any man may master the physical.
With enough knowledge, any man may become wise.
It is the true warrior who can master both ... and surpass the result.

Tien T'ai

In the martial arts, we refer to "the way" as *Budo*, which is interpreted in many ways but essentially refers to the seriousness of training and the spiritual path one follows to gain success and wisdom. It is the way of improving one's self in body, mind, and spirit. *Budo* is a way of life and must be practiced in all our affairs. *Budo* is the way of the warrior. With *Budo*, the point is not only to compete (in the martial arts), but to find peace and mastery of the self. It is concerned with cultivation of the mind and a reflection upon the nature of the self, the question: who am I?

So I can be successful in all my affairs, *Budo* is my way of life. This has been taught in the martial arts for centuries and still holds true today. When people first come into my karate academy, they are in their infancy. They are full of wonder, fear, and expectations—there is the belief that something special will be accomplished and that their lives will improve.

The new students try on their uniforms (*gi*) for the first time, which feels strange, yet exciting. Conquering their fear of attending their first class, they enter the *dojo* floor as a novice. If they have always wanted to try karate, the student conquers that initial fear and goes for it.

A student wears his white belt with pride and anticipation. In the first class, he learns that the "way of the warrior" is gained through the daily practice of *Budo*. He also learns that in order to achieve success, he must learn one step at a time, with there being eleven steps to reach the black belt level. Each step has its own techniques as well as physical and mental challenges, with these challenges increasing as a student advances through the ranks.

Just as in our daily lives, there are obstacles to contend with along the way to becoming a Black Belt. Life's issues, big and small, get in the way and challenge the student's resolve. As the student progresses, she is being trained to meet these challenges as a warrior: using *Budo* as her way, never giving up, and always maintaining focus on her purpose and goal.

At the level of a green belt (approximately one year), we begin to see the true nature and character of the student. Often, the student will quit (similar to what the student has done with many things in his life), become lazy and complacent, or begin to complain and whine about being bored or whatever. Fortunately, there are those who will meet this time as a challenge and fight to achieve their goals, as is the way of the warrior.

Nearly 50 percent of students will quit during this first year of training, and only 5 percent will ever reach black belt. This is the story of the masses. Given any challenge on the path to success, only 3–5 percent of people will do what it takes to succeed. This is a sad fact of life.

Unless you do your best, the day will come when,
tired and hungry, you will halt just short of the goal you were ordered to reach,
and by halting you will make useless the efforts and deaths of thousands.
General George S. Patton

The way of *Budo* requires us to meet challenges and opportunities with perseverance and determination. There is no room for quitting or retreat: you either do or you don't. Whine and cry, or stand up and fight.

From day one, a martial arts student is challenged and either stands tall and meets the challenge or she surrenders to her defects of character. This is the truth in her life both inside and outside of the *dojo*.

Success is a path that must be set upon with sound and solid resolve. The excuses and the whining must cease, and the way of the warrior must conquer. A brown belt who is testing to become a black belt has met all the tests of his resolve over a period of three to five years and is ready to achieve something that very few people ever achieve—a Black Belt.

I assure you, these students will have had challenges in their karate lives, personal lives, and business lives. They will have considered quitting a few times and had to weather injuries and pain. They will have gotten frustrated and failed along the way. They will have had others in their lives tell them to quit and that eventually they would fail, but through all of this, they did not quit—they persevered.

They followed the path of the warrior and they practiced *Budo*. Their dream and vision to achieve the level of black belt never failed them. Along the way, they remained teachable and humble. They were not intimated by the dream stealers and did not let the distractions in life detour them in their mission.

The path to black belt and the path to success in every other aspect of life are laid out by the steps and paths of those who have succeeded before us. Following their path assures us of success and freedom. Quitting is the path of the masses. Which do you choose?

*Do not seek to follow in the footsteps of the men of old;
seek the things they sought.*

Matsuo Basho

When a brown belt has successfully passed the tests and is being promoted to a professional black belt, we have a special ceremony. During this ceremony, it is traditional that we, as black belts, remember what it was like to struggle through the challenges in order to reach success. It is also critical that we have our "tea ceremony" that illustrates the very nature of life, *Budo*, success, and freedom. During our tea ceremony, we reflect on the lessons of *Budo* and share how we have carried this into our daily lives. We tell how we have struggled and failed and how we ultimately succeeded. We remember the feeling of being a white belt, and we renew our spirit.

As the ceremony continues, we fill our cups with tea until they overflow and cannot hold any more. This is a reflection of ourselves and how we become so full of self that we no longer are teachable. This creates a person who is driven by ego and not by the way of *Budo*. It creates arrogance and stops growth in body, mind, and spirit. As each of us spills off some of the tea from our cups, we once again return to the novice level and are ready to learn and progress to the next level. We have gained strength and wisdom, but we must remain on the path and the spirit of the warrior.

The lessons we learn from practicing *Budo* in all our affairs is critical to our success. When we allow outside issues to destroy our warrior spirit, our visions and dreams are lost. Every great warrior has seriousness within his or her soul that inspires and creates success and freedom.

Although it is important to study and train for skill in techniques,
for the man who wishes to truly accomplish the way of Budo,
it is more important to make his whole life in training and therefore
not training for skill and strength alone, but also for spiritual attainment.

Mas Oyama

By taking stock in our own lives and taking necessary action to become a warrior, we follow the path (*Budo*) for success. It is a path based on the principles for success, and these steps will work in all areas of our lives. Those of us who are willing to change, to become teachable, and to take action will see improvement immediately.

The Victor

If you think you are beaten, you are; if you think you dare not, you don't.
If you like to win, but you think you can't, it's almost a cinch that you won't.

If you think you'll lose, you're lost, for out in the world we find,
Success begins with a fellow's will. It's all in the state of mind.

If you think you are outclassed, you are; you've got to think high to rise.
You've got to be sure of yourself before you can ever win the prize.

Life's battles don't always go to the stronger or faster man;
But sooner or later the man who wins, is the man who thinks he can.

C. W. Longenecker

I am grateful that you have taken a moment in time to experience my message. My hope and my prayer is that you have related to something I have shared and that your life may be enhanced by the message of hope. I truly believe that all of us deserve the best that life has to offer as long as we live our lives with the warrior spirit and do the right thing.

Remember along the way of becoming a warrior ("one who serves") to be kind and inspire others, remain teachable, and become the teacher. Gain strength and wisdom through your failures and success, and practice *Budo* in all aspects of your life. We do for those who can't do for themselves—and we never, ever give up!

Chapter 22

Spirituality

Spirituality is a domain of awareness.

Deepak Chopra

How did I get from there to here? I have believed in a power greater than myself since I can remember. No matter what you believe or don't believe in, it is certainly your right. I can respect you for that.

Through my experiences over the last fifty-four years, I have come to believe there is a spirit watching over me; and once I made a decision to make a conscious contact with that spirit, my life has become a blessing. In my life, God is that spirit, but it might be different for you. I am simply referring to a power, a belief, or a value greater than self. Something that I cannot see, yet I can feel its presence. I know it is there because there have been many times in my life in which I was totally dependent physically, mentally, and spiritually upon something outside of myself.

This power, which I call God, has done for me what I couldn't do for myself. This spirit has given me direction for his will for me and the power to carry it out, the free will to live my life for evil or for good, and has provided consequences for my actions.

In 1984, I had gone to the Magic Castle in Hollywood to perform and to drink. I left the Castle at 2:00 AM and headed for home. I was drunk and in a blackout again. There was a flatbed truck parked on the side of the road, one block from my home, which I ran into at fifty-five miles an hour. The flatbed completely ripped off the top of my car, slicing my head severely.

I remember stepping out of the car, blood pouring from my head. I was stunned. This was not my first accident while driving drunk, but this time something was different. I had that moment of clarity that I spoke about earlier. As I stood in the middle of the street bleeding, I realized that I was completely powerless, full of shame, remorse, and fear—and I needed help.

I looked up into the heavens and covered my eyes with my bloody hands as I yelled, "God, please make this a dream. When I open my eyes, let me awake from this nightmare safe in my own bed!" I removed my hands from my eyes and all I could see and feel was blood, pain, and incomprehensible demoralization. As people surrounded me and tended to my wounds, I again looked to the heavens, and my prayer was simple and sincere: "I need help. I will do whatever it takes to change my life. Please, help me."

Had anyone else been in my car that evening, the person would have been decapitated! How was I able to drive night after night in a drunken stupor and not seriously injure or kill someone along the way? I know that there was a power greater than myself that was watching over me and those around me. I know today that my purpose in life is to carry the message of recovery to others.

I have come to believe that spirituality is within us all, and that it is transmitted through our actions and our deeds. I believe that my God speaks through others and guides my path in life if I choose to listen and take action. This power has blessed this world with beauty and wonders beyond our understanding.

I was brought up to believe I had complete power over my life so I didn't need help from anything or anyone. I was told I needed to fend for myself and row my own boat. This was a tremendous weight on my shoulders; and until I understood that all I had control over was my own actions and attitude, I struggled and suffered.

Having surrendered my life and my will over to the care of a power greater than myself, I have found a new freedom and been relieved from the bondage of self-will. My life was consumed by self-will run riot. I realized I have all the power necessary to be the best I can be, but I have no power over people, places, and things.

I must seek out my higher power's will for me and carry it out. Then, I have to be willing to accept the results. Today, I stay out of the "results" business and just take the next appropriate step towards my purpose in life. I can't focus on what needs to be changed in you or in others—it is none of my business. All I can do is make sure I am the best person I can be.

Acceptance is the key to all my problems. Lack of power and acceptance is my dilemma. Until I accepted people, places, and things for being exactly as they are supposed to be, I could not find peace. Until I began to focus on myself, rather than on changing others, I couldn't find serenity. Until I stopped trying to change my wife and merely accepted her for who and what she was, I couldn't love her fully. Until I changed *my* behavior in the marriage, nothing improved. Once I learned this lesson and began to change *me*, rather than "them," my life and the lives around me improved.

The personal life deeply lived always expands into truths beyond itself.

Anais Nin

We become the man or woman we have always wanted to be. We have a newfound freedom and acceptance. We find that our attitude is one of gratitude, rather than negativity. We find that fear and lack of faith will disappear, and that our higher power is doing for us what we couldn't do for ourselves. We will find serenity, and we will have peace.

To "let go" does not mean to stop caring;
it means I can't do it for someone else.
To "let go" is not to cut myself off;
it is the realization that I must not control another.
To "let go" is not to fix;
but to be supportive.
To "let go" is not to be in the middle arranging all the outcomes;
but to allow others to effect their destinies.
To "let go" is not to be protective;
it is to permit another to face reality.
To "let go" is not to regret the past;
but to grow and live for the future.
To "let go" is to fear less and love more.

Author Unknown

It is a blessing to be awake and aware of all the good in the world and in our ability to make a difference. It is time to be in the moment and to make this moment and the next moment a blessing.

One of his students asked Buddha, "Are you the messiah?"
"No," answered Buddha.
"Then are you a healer?"
"No," Buddha replied.
"Then are you a teacher?" the student persisted.
"No, I am not a teacher."
"Then what are you?" asked the student, exasperated.
"I am awake," Buddha replied.

I look up into the heavens, look at the mountains, the oceans, rivers, or stars, and with humility and an open mind and heart, I ask for guidance and help, and affirm that I am willing to take direction and change. Then I sit back, get quiet, and listen. The answers always come.

Below are things I do each and every day to keep myself in a conscious contact with a power greater than myself. This keeps me centered, focused, and right-size. I assure you that the spirit of the way is within your heart and soul just waiting for you to listen and take action.

Daily Necessities
(Tips and pointers for building a spiritual life from scratch)

Pray
Meditate
Be aware/Stay awake
Bow
Practice yoga
Feel
Chant and sing
Breathe and smile
Relax/Enjoy/Laugh/Play
Create/Envision
Let Go/Forgive/Accept
Walk/Exercise/Move
Work/Serve/Contribute
Listen/Learn/Enquire
Consider/Reflect
Cultivate oneself/Enhance competencies
Cultivate contentment
Cultivate flexibility
Cultivate friendship and collaboration
Lighten up
Celebrate and appreciate
Dream
Give thanks
Evolve
Love
Share/Give/Receive

Brad C. Wenneberg

Walk softly/Live gently
Expand/Radiate/Dissolve
Simplify
Surrender/Trust
Be born anew

from *Awakening the Buddha Within* by Lama Surya Das

God, grant me the serenity
to accept the things I cannot change;
courage to change the things I can;
and the wisdom to know the difference.

Reinhold Niebuhr

Chapter 23

Soar Like an Eagle

Did you know that an eagle knows when a storm is approaching long before it breaks? The eagle will fly to some high spot and wait for the winds to come. When the storm hits, it sets its wings so that the wind will pick it up and lift it above the storm. While the storm rages below, the eagle is soaring above it.

The eagle doesn't escape the storm—it simply uses the storm to lift it higher. It rises on the winds that bring the storm. When the storms of life come upon us—and all of us will experience them—we can rise above them by setting our minds and our belief toward our higher power, whom I choose to call God. The storms don't have to overcome us as we can allow God's power to lift us above them. This enables us to ride the winds of the storms that bring sickness, tragedy, failure, and disappointment into our lives. We can soar above the storm. Remember, if we are really honest with ourselves, it is not the burdens of life that weigh us down; it is how we handle them.

Author Unknown

It is no accident that the eagle is our national symbol of strength, peace, and wisdom. We are all meant to soar like an eagle, to find peace amidst the storm, to find serenity in the face of tragedy, and to achieve success and happiness. But it is not up to anyone to hand this to us—it is within our grasp if we take the right actions.

Life happens to all of us. Sometimes it seems that we are the only one experiencing the anguish of life. Sometimes we feel alone and abandoned. We have our ups and our downs, and at times life doesn't seem fair. We don't have to allow troubles and heartache to overcome us. We can rely on a power greater than self to help us through the tough times and allow us to soar like the eagles.

Our attitude and our beliefs can keep us soaring above the storm—or get us smacked right in the face with it. The attitude of a winner will see the cup half full and be willing to find the positive in the middle of a crisis. It is our choice to soar or to be a victim.

We must refuse to be a victim and fight back, do whatever it takes to soar like an eagle. We must stand up and be the very best we can be, and don't allow the negatives in life to beat us down. We must stop all those dream stealers in their tracks and deny anyone the right to take away our hopes and our purpose.

With everything we have, we must stand for what is good and what is right. We must stand for our freedom and our right to be successful. We must refuse to buy into the doom and gloomers in our society. We should stick with the winners and live to learn. When someone or something stands in the way of our dreams, we should step around or over them. We are passionate and determined to go where the eagles go even during the toughest of times. We have stopped blaming and stopped whining. We are warriors!

I have shared with you my story; and as you can see, I have lived two entirely different lives in one lifetime. I spent many years of my life as a self-centered, self-will running riot, ego- driven liar, drunk, and thief. I abused my rights as a human, and I hurt those around me. I was miserable and deserved nothing but heartache. As a result of my lifestyle, I became a broken- down shallow of a man—the complete opposite of a warrior!

My second life has been lived with honor, humility, honesty, kindness, and spirit of the warrior. I have made my amends, and I have continued to act my way into better living. I treat others with respect, and I accept them for who and what they are. I take care of my mind, body, and spirit.

I am a teacher *and* a student. I carry the message of hope to everyone I meet, and I focus on solutions and not problems. I am kind and loving towards those I meet, and I am gracious to those in need. I am sober and awake to all that life has to offer. I have positive self-esteem, and I will fight for my right to be happy and free.

I don't run from issues of life—I deal with them as they come about, and I seek guidance from my mentors and my higher power. I stand tall and accept responsibility for my mistakes, and I am humbled by my successes. I don't condemn your success or wish you ill as I pray for everyone's well-being, success, and happiness.

It doesn't matter where we have come from or what we have or haven't done in our lifetimes—we can turn our lives around. We must decide to soar like an eagle and fight for a better and more fulfilling life.

I have been challenged in every aspect of my life, much of which I have shared with you in this book. It is up to me to take action and make changes. The only person who was stopping me from succeeding was me and me alone. It doesn't matter if we are young or old, well or sick—each and every moment of our life is in our hands. We must embrace life and seize the moments, and then we must live our lives as warriors!

We all die. The goal isn't to live forever.
The goal is to create something that will.

Chuck Palahniuk

I choose to soar like an eagle wise and strong
Above the storm directed toward happiness and success and of the "way."
I refuse to give in and stop soaring.
I am worth the effort. I have much to offer the world.
You cannot stop my flight nor can you disable my will.
I will be successful and happy.
I will pass the message to others.
The message of the warrior and of the eagle will live on
generation after generation!

Shihan Brad C. Wenneberg

About the Author

Brad C. Wenneberg was born and raised mostly in Southern California, but lived for two years in Northern California and graduated high school there. He then attended Golden West and Fullerton colleges in Southern California and graduated with an AA Degree in Police Science. Brad also graduated from the Fullerton College Police Academy in 1973 and worked as a patrol officer for Anaheim Police Department until mid-1978. After a medical retirement from the police force, he worked for twelve years in the insurance industry as a broker and became a top salesman, earning a spot on the Million Dollar Round Table.

In 1992, Brad opened a karate studio, American Martial Arts Academy, in Fullerton, California. Now a 15,000-square-foot, million-dollar business with more than 500 students, the academy has empowered thousands of people over the past sixteen years to maximize their potential. Brad is the Shihan/Master Instructor, as well as the owner along with his wife, Bonnie, of AMAA. Brad and Bonnie are also entrepreneurs with their leadership development and marketing business, B&B Enterprises, which allows them to assist, mentor and train others to be business owners with multiple streams of income. Their two adult children, Sheri and Jason, work alongside their parents in these endeavors, and all four enjoy playing and traveling together.

Free Bonus for *Unleash Your Inner Warrior*

Get Your Free Bonus E-Book: "5 Ways to Find Your Warrior Purpose"

What do you want out of life? More important, how are you going to get there?

Simply put, all of your hopes and dreams begin with a purpose. That purpose will serve as the guiding principle to help you accomplish anything you set your mind to—as long as you are willing to abandon old ways of thinking and commit to creating abundance and joy in your life.

Through five simple steps, Brad C. Wenneberg reveals the core principles of success that will allow you to begin living the life of your dreams *now*. Commit to these success principles in your own life, and you, too, can get everything you desire!

Get your free bonus e-book at
www.unleashyourinnerwarrior.com

BUY A SHARE OF THE FUTURE IN YOUR COMMUNITY

These certificates make great holiday, graduation and birthday gifts that can be personalized with the recipient's name. The cost of one S.H.A.R.E. or one square foot is $54.17. The personalized certificate is suitable for framing and will state the number of shares purchased and the amount of each share, as well as the recipient's name. The home that you participate in "building" will last for many years and will continue to grow in value.

Here is a sample SHARE certificate:

THIS CERTIFIES THAT
YOUR NAME HERE
HAS INVESTED IN A HOME FOR A DESERVING FAMILY

1985-2005

TWENTY YEARS OF BUILDING FUTURES IN OUR COMMUNITY ONE HOME AT A TIME

1200 SQUARE FOOT HOUSE @ $65,000 = $54.17 PER SQUARE FOOT
This certificate represents a tax deductible donation. It has no cash value.

YES, I WOULD LIKE TO HELP!

I support the work that Habitat for Humanity does and I want to be part of the excitement! As a donor, I will receive periodic updates on your construction activities but, more importantly, I know my gift will help a family in our community realize the dream of homeownership. **I would like to SHARE in your efforts against substandard housing in my community!** *(Please print below)*

PLEASE SEND ME _____ SHARES at $54.17 EACH = $ $_____

In Honor Of: _____

Occasion: (Circle One)   HOLIDAY   BIRTHDAY   ANNIVERSARY

　　　OTHER: _____

Address of Recipient: _____

Gift From: _____ *Donor Address:* _____

Donor Email: _____

I AM ENCLOSING A CHECK FOR $ $_____ PAYABLE TO HABITAT FOR HUMANITY OR PLEASE CHARGE MY VISA OR MASTERCARD *(CIRCLE ONE)*

Card Number _____ Expiration Date: _____

Name as it appears on Credit Card _____ Charge Amount $ _____

Signature _____

Billing Address _____

Telephone # Day _____ Eve _____

PLEASE NOTE: Your contribution is tax-deductible to the fullest extent allowed by law.
Habitat for Humanity • P.O. Box 1443 • Newport News, VA 23601 • 757-596-5553
www.HelpHabitatforHumanity.org